BONDS

AN INTRODUCTION TO THE CORE CONCEPTS

BONDS

AN INTRODUCTION TO THE CORE CONCEPTS

Mark Mobius

WILEY

John Wiley & Sons Singapore Pte. Ltd.

Published in 2012 by John Wiley & Sons Singapore Pte. Ltd. 1 Fusionopolis Walk, #07-01, Solaris South Tower, Singapore 138628.

Other Wiley Editorial Offices

John Wiley & Sons, 111 River Street, Hoboken, NJ 07030, USA
John Wiley & Sons, The Atrium, Southern Gate, Chichester, West Sussex, P019 8SQ, United Kingdom
John Wiley & Sons (Canada) Ltd., 5353 Dundas Street West, Suite 400, Toronto, Ontario, M9B 6HB, Canada
John Wiley & Sons Australia Ltd., 42 McDougall Street, Milton, Queensland 4064, Australia
Wiley-VCH, Boschstrasse 12, D-69469 Weinheim, Germany

ISBN 978–0–470–82147–3 (Cloth)
ISBN 978–1–118–33941–1 (ePDF)
ISBN 978–1–118–33942–8 (Mobi)
ISBN 978–1–118–33943–5 (ePub)

Typeset in 11/13 Galliard-Roman by MPS Limited, Chennai, India
Printed in Singapore by Markono Print Media Pte Ltd

10 9 8 7 6 5 4 3 2 1

CONTENTS

ACKNOWLEDGMENTS

If I were to attempt to acknowledge all the wonderful people who helped formulate the ideas that went into this book it would take many pages. Suffice to say that I have learned a great deal from the thousands of people working in and studying emerging markets since I started this adventure in the 1970s even before I started managing the Templeton Emerging Markets Fund. Over the years, experts within the Franklin Resources organization have helped the Templeton Emerging Markets Group grow enormously in assets under management, and instead of only five countries in which to invest in 1987 with only US$100 million, we now cover over 60 countries with tens of billions of dollars invested.

Special thanks go to Shalini Dadlani for her excellent research and editing as well as the team at Wiley who have helped bring this project to fruition. Of course I must take sole responsibility for any errors and omissions.

Mark Mobius
Executive Chairman of Templeton Emerging Markets Group

1

AN INTRODUCTION TO BONDS

When people talk about investing, they often utter the words "stocks and bonds" in the same breath. The two go together like "bread and butter." But as soon as the conversation shifts to the latest glamour stocks, the subject of bonds often gets lost in the shuffle.

Compared to the more volatile ups and downs of stocks, bonds are, generally, steady, conservative investments that pay interest and return the principal at maturity. They are also called fixed income securities or debt instruments.

If stocks are perceived as being the focus of attention at the conversational level, on a global level the amount actually invested in bonds far exceeds that of stocks. Figures from TheCityUK show that the worldwide value of all bonds outstanding was a record US$95 trillion in 2010, with about US$35 trillion in the U.S. bond market. This contrasts with US$47.8 trillion for global equity-market capitalization in the same year, according to data gathered by the World Federation of Exchanges and various stock exchanges globally. Looked at from another perspective, the value of bonds outstanding worldwide is about five times the current gross domestic product of the United States. From 1990 to the first quarter of 2007, the global bond market mushroomed in size by 313 percent. So, clearly, interest in bonds is stronger than it has ever been. The three main attractions of bonds are that they provide:

1. Predictable income streams
2. Capital preservation
3. Portfolio diversification

At one time, the relative safety of bonds led some to dub them—somewhat cavalierly—as an investment vehicle for widows and orphans. More commonly, they became a favorite of the rich. The phrase "clipping coupons" entered the vernacular as a reference to a bond's interest payments. Years ago, bonds came with a set of coupons that could be detached and periodically redeemed for cash. These were called bearer bonds, and the coupons were the sole proof of ownership. The term "clipping coupons" still lingers, even though all bonds issued in the United States since 1983 have been registered, meaning that the owner's name is recorded so that interest payments can be mailed. Registration also helps tax authorities keep track of tax collections. Many international bonds, however, are still in bearer form.

Today, institutional investors such as banks and pension funds represent the majority of bondholders. Individual investors, however, maintain a fairly firm grip on the bond market. Their participation is expected to increase as baby boomers reach retirement age and seek investments that offer both income and investment stability.

THE HISTORY OF BONDS

Bonds have a storied history dating back to the thirteenth century, when the Venetian government issued the Venetian *prestiti*, which was designed to pay 5 percent interest twice a year *forever* but never actually mature. In other words, the principal was never paid back. (Even the interest payments stopped in the fifteenth century when Venice was decimated by wars with the Turks.) The *prestiti* concept proved so successful that as England and France rose to power they issued their own perpetual bonds, called *consols* and *rentes*, respectively.

In the United States after the Civil War, corporate bonds helped finance the railroad-building boom (some of which defaulted leaving bondholders in the lurch). Bonds reached their heyday during World War II when the U.S. government raised almost US$200 billion in war bonds to help propel the Allies to victory. They have been and are the main instrument for financing economic growth and development on an international scale.

Bonds started to become more available to smaller investors in the 1980s. A series of laws deregulating financial markets resulted in many bonds being packaged into much more affordable denominations than the US$10,000, US$50,000, or even US$100,000 minimums that had previously been the norm. Suddenly, the small investors had a chance to rub shoulders with the wealthy and the big institutions who were the main players in the bond market.

BOND ESSENTIALS

Bonds are basically long-term IOUs between a borrower and a lender. When a government, corporation, agency, or other entity needs to raise capital for business expansion or for infrastructure projects such as roads, schools, and airports, they borrow money from investors.

Investors who purchase a bond are essentially loaning money to these issuers for a fixed period of time. In return, investors receive a promise that they will receive interest payments at certain intervals and also have their principal returned on a stated future date.

The details are spelled out in a contract called the bond *indenture*, which is a legally binding document. The indenture can be quite lengthy and extremely tedious to read, but it is important because it contains all the relevant facts about the bond issue.

These include information about the type of the bond, the size of the issue, the terms, the financial backing for the issue, provisions that protect the investor, call privileges, and the appointment of a trustee to represent bondholders. Should the issuer fail to live up to the terms of the contract, bondholders are entitled to pursue legal remedies.

The bond business is rife with jargon and terminology. The basic terms are explained below (adapted from www.investopedia.com). For a fuller, more comprehensive list, see the Glossary.

Face Value (or Par Value)

This is the dollar value of a bond that is to be repaid at maturity. In other words, this is what the investor has loaned to the issuer and will get back. Generally, bonds are issued in denominations of US$1,000, but some can be in denominations of US$5,000 or even larger.

Coupon Rate

This is the amount of interest, stated in percentage terms, the bond is going to pay on a quarterly, semiannual, or annual basis. This rate remains in effect for the life of the bond even as the bond's price fluctuates. For example, a US$1,000 bond with a 10 percent coupon paid annually earns US$100 in interest each year. That same bond with a 10 percent coupon paid semiannually earns US$50 twice a year. Most bonds pay interest semiannually. The former method of clipping coupons has been largely replaced by an automated system where interest is mailed directly to the registered bondholder or deposited in investment accounts.

Receiving a dependable stream of income from regular interest payments is one of the attractions of investing in bonds. But not all bonds subscribe to this fixed-payout formula. Some bonds pay a floating rate of interest, where the rate is adjusted periodically in line with some measure of market rates, such as the rate on Treasury bills. This means the bond always pays interest that is at least in the ballpark of prevailing interest rates. The major risk with this type of bond has to do with changes to the financial health of the issuer. The interest rate floats only in response to interest-rate conditions; it has nothing to do with the issuer's creditworthiness.

Zero-coupon bonds do not make periodic interest payments but, rather, pay their interest in a lump sum at maturity. Zeros are sold at deep discounts to their face value, such as US$650 for a US$1,000 bond. At maturity, the full US$1,000 is paid, reflecting the amount that was originally paid and the interest that has accumulated over time.

Maturity Date

This is the date on which the principal is paid back. The last interest payment is also made on that date. Bonds feature a range of maturities, from 1 day to 30 years. Short-term bonds are those that mature in 2 years or less; intermediate bonds have maturities of up to 10 years, while long-term bonds are 10 years or longer.

Price

A bond's price is not simply a matter of quoting its face value, because if the bond is traded on the secondary market before it reaches maturity, the price is affected by the rise or fall of interest rates and credit quality.

An important rule to bear in mind is that when market interest rates go up, bond prices go down, and vice versa. For example, if you have a 10-year US$1,000 bond that pays a coupon rate of 5 percent and market interest rates suddenly fall to 4 percent, a bond with a 5 percent coupon rate looks more attractive (like finding a bank that pays a higher interest rate on a savings account), and people will pay more than the face value to buy it—US$1,081.04, in fact. Selling it would produce a capital gain of US$81.04. (A bond that sells above par value is called a *premium* bond.)

On the other hand, if market interest rates rise to 6 percent, a 5 percent coupon rate loses some of its appeal, and the price of the bond declines to US$926.39—a capital loss of US$73.61. (A bond selling below par value is termed a *discount* bond.) We will look more closely at the mathematics of bonds in a later chapter. For now, it's enough to say that any adjustment in price fully reflects the impact of the new market interest rate and makes the value of the bond equivalent to others paying a coupon at the higher or lower market rate.

Yield

There are three kinds of yields that investors need to be concerned about—the coupon yield, the current yield, and the yield to maturity. The coupon yield is simply the interest rate on a bond promised by the issuer, expressed in percentage form. In our example above, the coupon yield on the US$1,000 bond is 10 percent. This allows investors to calculate their interest payments over the life of the bond.

The current yield is the bond's annual coupon payment divided by its market price. If a US$1,000 par-value bond with a 10 percent coupon is selling for US$950 in the secondary market, the current yield is US$100/$950 = 10.52 percent. This is useful for providing a rough estimate of the return on an investment if a bond was purchased at something other than par.

The yield to maturity is a truer measure of a bond's total return because it looks at several factors, such as principal, interest, and the time to redemption. This is the one that most people refer to when they mention "yield." The yield to maturity takes into account the difference between what was paid for the bond in the secondary market and its redemption value at maturity. Obviously, this doesn't apply if the bond was purchased at par value. It also considers the amount earned from reinvesting the bond's coupon income over time and the effect that compounding can have on the return.

Seniority

Like preferred stock, bonds are regarded as senior securities. This means that paying interest on bonds receives a higher priority than dividends paid to common stockholders. If the bond issuer runs into financial trouble, bondholders (who are creditors) rank ahead of common stockholders when a company's assets are distributed.

Sinking Fund

Bonds can be repaid at maturity but can also be redeemed in part or in their entirety before that date. Early repayment is often handled through a sinking fund. This is a special account into which money is deposited and managed by the bond trustee, who uses the funds to pay off portions of the bond issue. Having such a fund is reassuring and helps minimize the risk of the issuer not being able to repay the principal when it comes due. Details of the sinking fund can be found in the *indenture*.

Call Provisions

These allow the issuer to buy back, or call, part or all of the bond issue before maturity. The most common reason for repurchasing bonds early is that interest rates have dropped and the issuer wants to save money on the coupon payments by reissuing bonds at the lower market interest rate. Generally, the call price is above the bond's par value. The call premium, as the difference in price is known, is designed to placate bondholders who might not be very happy about losing the higher coupon rate. Lower coupon rates can affect the bondholder's yield to maturity. Call provisions can kick in within a few years of the bond being issued, but some bonds have what is known as a deferred call provision, which means they cannot be called for a certain period of time—say, the first 10 years.

Negative Covenant

A bond covenant preventing certain activities, unless agreed to by the bondholders. Negative covenants are written directly into the agreement creating the bond issue, are legally binding on the issuer, and exist to protect the best interests of the bondholders. This arrangement is also referred to as a restrictive covenant. Think of a negative covenant as a promise not to do something. Usually, negative covenants limit the amount of dividends a firm can pay to shareholders and restrict the ability of the firm to issue additional debt. Generally, the more negative covenants exist in a bond issue, the lower the interest rate on the debt will be since the restrictive covenants make the bonds safer in the eyes of investors.

Affirmative Covenant

This is a type of promise or contract that requires a party to do something. For example, a bond covenant that provides that the issuer will maintain adequate levels of insurance or deliver audited financial statements is an affirmative covenant. Affirmative (or positive) covenants can be compared to restrictive (or negative) covenants, which require a party not to do something, such as sell certain assets. In bond agreements, both affirmative and restrictive covenants are used to protect the interests of both issuer and bondholder.

Protective Covenant

This affords bondholders legal protections by limiting issuers from taking certain actions during the life of the bond. Negative covenants prohibit an issuer from doing certain things and positive covenants specify that actions must be taken or conditions fulfilled. An example of the former might be not allowing a company that has issued corporate bonds to issue further long-term debt. As for the latter, the covenant might demand that assets be maintained in good condition.

STOCKS VERSUS BONDS

Between 1870 and 1940, stocks and bonds posted approximately equivalent returns. It has only been since World War II that stocks have outstripped bonds in total returns. From the postwar period until recent years, the long-term return on all bonds was only about half that of stocks. When inflation is factored in, the real return was more like one-third.

If those results seem disappointing, other considerations favor bonds. Bonds may not have soared as high as stocks but neither have they nose-dived as badly as stocks. After the stock market crash of 1929 that ushered in the Great Depression, stocks posted their worst year in 1931, with a loss of 43.13 percent. The worst year for bonds was 1969 when they lost 8.13 percent. Stocks rebounded in 1933 with a gain of 54.20 percent, while bonds had their best year in 1982, with a rise of 32.62 percent.

Bonds tend to be safer and less volatile than stocks, but this doesn't mean they are absolutely safe. Only U.S. government securities such as Treasury bills, notes, and bonds are risk-free. Thousands of other bonds on

the market issued by corporations and financial institutions range from top-of-the line investment-grade bonds to higher-yield, speculative issues ("junk bonds"). However, investors should derive some comfort in knowing that the global default rate on investment-grade bonds has been less than 1 percent for the past 20 years.

When major bond defaults do occur, they attract attention. One of the largest defaults in history dates back to the Russian Revolution of 1917 and its overthrow of the czarist regime. When the regime came to an end, billions of rubles worth of bonds suddenly became virtually worthless. During Argentina's severe economic crisis of 2001–2002, the country could only manage to pay 25 cents on the dollar on its US$90 billion outstanding bond debt.

In the United States, recent corporate bond defaults have included airlines such as Delta and Northwest and energy-trading company Enron. General Motors and Ford have both seen their bonds downgraded from investment grade to speculative grade. Only one major city since the Great Depression has actually defaulted on its bonds—Cleveland in 1978. A few years earlier, New York City came close to default but was saved by a massive federal bailout.

BOND FUNCTIONS

Governments, public agencies, and corporations all have reasons for issuing bonds. Contrary to what many might think, government tax revenues (income tax, sales tax, gasoline tax, and so on) and fees are not sufficient to fund the many public services that are now taken for granted. Issuing a bond allows a government to quickly raise the needed sums for a new school or road project, for example, without having to resort to raising taxes. With about US$8 trillion in outstanding debt, the U.S. Department of the Treasury maintains the distinction of being the world's biggest bond market.

Bonds allow corporations to rapidly raise billions to finance everything from new acquisitions to new capital equipment. They offer an alternative to issuing new stock, which might not be welcomed by stockholders for two reasons. If demand for the company's stock remained essentially the same, more shares would dilute existing stockholders' equity and could even cause the stock's price to decline. Corporations also gain tax benefits from issuing bonds that wouldn't apply to new stock. Interest payments to bondholders allow companies to claim a pretax deduction on the interest expense, thus reducing their overall tax bill.

WHAT DO BONDS OFFER?

All investments carry some risk, but some investments are riskier than others. When people refer to the risk of an investment, they are talking about whether they might lose money. For bonds traded on the secondary market (and not held to maturity), this could mean a loss of principal if changes in market interest rates cause the bond's price to depreciate. The return is the possibility of making money. With stocks, this refers to both capital appreciation when a stock's price goes up and to dividends that shareholders receive. A bond's return reflects its interest payments and any appreciation in its price from interest-rate movements—again this applies only if the bonds are traded. However, as a general rule, the return potential of bonds is rather modest compared with other investments.

So why are bonds such popular investments? One reason is that, unlike stocks, they allow investors to sleep at night because there are no stomach-churning, roller-coaster rides in prices to worry about. During uncertain economic times or when a recession is looming, investors typically flock to the safe haven of bonds. The most attractive quality of bonds is their regular payment stream. For retirees or others needing a predictable source of income, a bond's interest payments provide a comforting level of security. If a major expense is on the horizon—say, a down payment on a house or college tuition—knowing that the principal will be returned on a particular date allows for prudent financial planning. This is especially true of the short-term (less than two years) cash needs for investors who can't risk losing capital. In such a case, if the stock market experiences a sudden downturn, there might not be enough time to recover financially to pay a big bill.

Many investors also try to align their bond maturities to meet future expenses. Even for those who don't need to rely on the income from their bonds, the amount of interest paid can be invested in the stock market or in new bonds on a schedule that takes advantage of dollar-cost averaging. With bonds as an anchor for a portfolio, an investor may feel more comfortable taking on greater risk with other investible assets in hopes of achieving a greater return.

Bonds also offer an excellent means of diversifying a portfolio. Every savvy investor has heard about the importance of diversification; that is, spreading risk over various kinds of assets—stocks, bonds, and cash. This is a safe investment strategy. Diversification can reduce risk as well as improve a portfolio's overall rate of return if the assets within it are uncorrelated. What this means is that the stocks in a portfolio should behave differently from the bonds in the portfolio, given similar market conditions. As one goes up, the other goes down and vice versa. The key to diversification is building a portfolio of several asset classes, which, over the long term, may produce favorable returns but do not move in the same direction at the same time.

Because bonds are fixed-income investments, inflation is always a paramount concern since it can easily erode any gains. As prices creep higher, purchasing power declines. Inflation is the bane of anyone living on a fixed income. The aim of investing is to earn a return that at least keeps pace with inflation. Investors should make a point of calculating their real returns, rather than simply relying on what the bond's coupon rate pays. Real return is calculated by subtracting the inflation rate (say, 3 percent) from the nominal or stated return (say, a bond with a coupon rate of 5 percent)—(5% − 3% = 2%). Those who like to gamble with their money might well sniff at a bond's real return. But everyone has heard tales of gamblers who ended up losing all their money. Thanks to the power of compounding on reinvested income payments, even small real returns can add up to a considerable amount over time.

The fixed-income universe offers a vast expanse of choices for the discerning investor. Literally thousands of bond issues are available, each with its own yields, maturities, and risk characteristics—from the most conservative to the most adventurous. Many short-term and long-term bonds can be bought and sold easily, but not all bonds are tradable, and some smaller issues may lack liquidity. The latter problem can be avoided by sticking to government bonds or those of well-known corporations.

However, there is no one single strategy for investing in bonds and no best way to time the market for the best return. Devising an appropriate strategy starts with investors thoroughly evaluating their personal needs and financial resources. This includes making an honest assessment of the level of risk that can be tolerated, taking into account such things as age, family situation, and existing debt. Bonds are not get-rich-quick financial instruments and can be complicated to understand. They are best for investors who are not looking for spectacular growth, but who, by temperament or financial situation, are content with earning a steady income and knowing that their original investment, if they have done their homework and chosen a creditworthy bond, will be returned to them at a fixed time.

SUMMARY

Bonds, also referred to as fixed-income securities or debt instruments, are loans made by investors to governments, financial institutions, corporations, and other entities for a fixed period of time. In return for these loans, investors receive regular interest payments and the return of their principal on the maturity date.

The history of bonds dates back to thirteenth-century Venice, and they have been used to raise money for economic growth and development around the world. They pay for new roads, schools, factories, corporate acquisitions, and more.

Stocks and bonds once had nearly equivalent returns but bonds have lagged behind stocks in the years since World War II. Inflation can also chip away at gains from fixed-income investments such as bonds, although the bond market is actually much larger than that of stocks. The advantages of bonds are that they are less volatile than equities, they offer a regular schedule of interest payments, the principal is returned on the maturity date, and they provide investment diversification. The best strategy for investing in bonds takes into account an investor's personal needs, investment resources, and tolerance for risk. Bonds have a role to play in everyone's portfolio.

QUICK QUIZ

1. What are the major benefits of investing in bonds?
2. Why do governments and corporations choose to issue bonds instead of using alternative means of financing?
3. For what types of financial goals would investing in bonds be most appropriate?
4. What kind of bond investment strategy works best?

2
BOND MARKETS

When people talk about "capital markets," they are usually referring to many different kinds of financial markets but mainly money markets, equity markets, and bond markets.

Money markets consist of financial institutions and dealers who buy, sell, borrow, and lend cash instruments and short-term financial instruments with durations from overnight to up to 12 months.

Equity markets refer to markets where equities or company stocks or stock derivatives are traded. Investors who own stocks or shares have an ownership share in the company. They may also receive dividends, which are payments to stockholders from a firm's earnings.

Bond markets are those in which participants buy and sell debt securities. As explained in Chapter 1, bonds are loans lasting from 12 months to over 30 years that normally pay interest at regular intervals and with repayment of their principal on the maturity date. Bond markets are also known as debt, credit, or fixed-income markets.

In all three, money is raised for various activities and exchanged between borrowers, lenders, owners, and investors. In the case of bond markets, the borrowers are the issuers of the bonds. They can be governments, corporations, banks, international organizations, individuals, and others. Lenders are the entities that lend through buying the bonds and securities.

BOND MARKET OPERATIONS

Domestic bond markets handle all types of debt, such as government securities and corporate issues, issued in their own domestic currency. These bonds are subject to the tax laws and regulations of their home governments. In the United States, the regulator is the Securities and Exchange Commission. In Hong Kong, the Securities and Futures Commission has the authority and in Japan, it's the Financial Services Agency. Some examples of domestic bond issuers are General Electric (United States), Barclays Bank (United Kingdom) and Électricité de France (France). Some of the largest government securities are issued by the U.S. government with its U.S. Treasuries, the Japanese Government with its JGBs or Japanese Government Bonds, and the United Kingdom government with its UK Treasuries or gilts.

If a domestic market is too small or too restrictive to meet an organization's needs, the international bond market offers an alternative. The most prominent of international bonds are Eurobonds. These are bonds that are denominated in a currency different from the currency of the country where the bond is issued or traded. The important point is that Eurobonds are outside the jurisdiction of the central bank that issues the currency in which the bond is denominated. For example, a U.S. dollar bond issued and traded in Germany would be considered a Eurobond. Eurobonds are important for multinational corporations since they enable those companies to raise money in the various countries in which they operate. A Japanese company, for example, may issue a Eurobond in Switzerland denominated in Euros. Note that the name is a little misleading. Eurobonds don't necessarily need to be issued in the euro currency. The reference to "euro" has to do with any deposits outside the purview of the domestic central bank. International bonds such as Eurobonds, Dragon Bonds, and others are discussed in Chapter 5.

The entire global bond market valued at over US$10 trillion includes Eurobonds and other types of bonds. There are a number of different types of international bonds. Foreign bonds, for example, are issued by foreign companies or governments and denominated in the currency of the issuing domestic market. Dragon Bonds are issued in Asia but usually denominated in U.S. dollars.

In recent years the world's largest issues of bonds were the United States with about 35 percent of the total, Europe with about 28 percent, and Japan with 13 percent.

OVER-THE-COUNTER (OTC) TRADING

The domestic and international bond markets consist of a large interconnected network of dealers and traders all over the world. Unlike the days of old when gesticulating traders, paper-strewn floors, and open outcry were the hallmarks of trading on exchanges, most bond trading now takes place electronically. Transactions are conducted between broker-dealers and large institutions over the counter. In OTC trades, traders deal directly with one another by telephone, facsimile, or computer, rather than on a physical exchange trading floor.

The sheer size of the bond market is one reason why it is so decentralized. Bear in mind that each corporation with one common stock issue outstanding could have multiple notes and bond issues on the market. And this doesn't even include the enormous number of government bond issues. The bond market dwarfs the global equity market.

Another reason for the decentralized nature of the market is that of the thousands of bond issues on the market at any given time, no two bond issues are identical. However, some bond trading still takes place on established exchanges, such as the New York Stock Exchange (NYSE)—the largest centralized bond market in the United States—and the London Stock Exchange (LSE).

Practically every government and the vast majority of the world's major corporations rely on bonds as a dependable tool for raising funds. The fixed-income market is attractive because it offers a range of instruments for organizations that need to borrow money for different purposes and periods of time.

For corporations, it can be faster and cheaper to issue bonds than to issue stock. Bonds do not dilute ownership percentages as new stock would. The interest that corporations pay on bonds can also be less costly than dividends. In the case of governments, which cannot issue equity, bonds offer an alternative to raising taxes or fees.

CASE STUDY: BOND TRADING ON THE NEW YORK STOCK EXCHANGE (NYSE)

Although the NYSE is most famous for stock or equity trading, it is also home to the largest centralized bond market in the United States. A wide range of bonds are traded on that market, including corporate, agency, and government bonds with corporate bond or other corporate debt issues accounting for the largest volume. Bond trading existed in the United States, before the founding of the NYSE in 1792, when a group of investors met under a buttonwood tree at what is now 68 Wall Street and made an agreement to trade securities on a commission basis. The new U.S. federal government had issued bonds a few years earlier in order to finance the Revolutionary War. The first securities that the group of investors traded included three government bonds and two bank stocks. From that time trading in various types of bonds increased so much so that in the 1800s New York State issued bonds to finance the Erie Canal, which linked the port of New York to the Great Lakes in the interior of the country. Over 4,000 bonds are now traded in the NYSE. The NYSE Bonds Trading Platform was launched in 2007 to provide more efficient and transparent computerized market pricing and trading information with an all-electronic design. That platform can handle 200,000 quotes per second. At the NYSE bonds are traded in three continuous trading sessions: early trading (4 A.M. to 9:30 A.M.), core trading (9:30 A.M. to 4 P.M.) and late trading (4 P.M. to 8 P.M.).

Source: NYSE website (www.nyse.com/bonds).

CASE STUDY: BOND TRADING AT THE LONDON STOCK EXCHANGE (LSE)

The LSE's history goes back over 300 years and is best known for its stock trading but the exchange also offers issuers of debt access to one of the largest pools of capital in the world, with over 15,000 debt securities listed on the exchange worth over US$15 trillion. Trading of debt securities on the LSE ranges from simple Eurobonds to complex asset-backed issues, high-yield bonds, and convertible or exchangeable bonds. Issuers include governments and their agencies, large corporations, and supranational bodies, such as the European Bank for Reconstruction and Development.

The listing of debt on the LSE involves two stages. First, the prospectus, or listing particulars, needs to be approved by the UK Listing Authority (UKLA). The UKLA assigns a reader who is responsible for checking the application, and if approved the issue is put on the Official List. In addition, a specialist Central Debt Desk is responsible for fast-tracking the documentation for new debt securities. Once the debt issue is put on the Official List, there is a normally short process to approve it for trading. Debt may be listed either on the exchange's Main Market or the Professional Securities Market. The Main Market provides issuers of debt to Europe's largest reservoirs of capital as well as wide exposure to financial-market experts. The Professional Securities Market is for issuers who want to report their financial statements in their own country's local accounting standards rather than internationally accepted standards and also allows more flexibility regarding the denomination and financial requirements. In order to give smaller retail investors the opportunity to trade, in 2010 the LSE set up its Order Book for Retail Bonds offering continuous two-way pricing for trading in UK gilts and retail-size corporate bonds. The system enables small amounts of trading and simplifies trading in bonds for retail investors in the UK.

Source: London Stock Exchange (www.londonstockexchange.com).

It must be noted that in emerging economies, bond markets are developing rapidly. Such countries as Brazil, India, China, Korea, and others have requirements for bonds, and thus markets are needed. In India, for example, the bond market began to develop in 1992, when India introduced a wide-ranging package of financial reforms. Before then, the government raised money from a captive group of banks at pre-announced coupon rates. There was no bond trading on an exchange. In 1995 a system of primary dealers or market makers was established, which helped produce a vibrant secondary market for government bonds. Plentiful credit disbursed by domestic banks and a preference by corporations to raise debt overseas rather than in India's domestic capital markets have caused the corporate debt market to lag behind the government bond market, but recently the corporate market has benefited from innovative bond issuances or such instruments as floating-rate instruments, zero-coupon bonds, convertible bonds, callable/putable bonds, and step-redemption bonds (which pay progressively higher rates of interest as maturity approaches) among others.

MARKET PLAYERS

The bond market includes three main players: issuers, investors, and intermediaries:

Issuers: These are the organizations (governments, companies, and others) that are looking to borrow money. Since the requirements of these organizations can often exceed the bank's appetite or willingness to lend, large bond issues are a good alternative for the borrowers. The main issuers of bonds include banks and other financial institutions, corporations (such as Procter & Gamble and Siemens), governments and quasi-government bodies (such as the Federal Home Loan Mortgage Corporation—Freddie Mac), and supranational organizations (such as the Inter-American Development Bank and the World Bank).

Investors: Individuals or institutions that provide capital to bond issuers. In return for loaning funds, investors expect a return on their money (interest) and repayment of their principal on a specified future date. Institutions such as insurance companies, mutual funds, pension funds, and savings institutions dominate the bond market and account for about 80 percent of bond holdings globally. Institutions want to include bonds in their portfolios because of their predictable income flow, large size, and liquidity.

Intermediaries: These market players bring issuers and investors together. Merchant banks, investment banks, financial advisers, and brokers function as intermediaries and play a vital role in the bond market not only during the issuing primary market stage but also in the trading secondary market stage.

In the United States, market intermediaries for U.S. Treasuries are banks and securities broker-dealers that deal in U.S. government securities with the Federal Reserve Bank of New York, one of 12 regional Reserve Banks in the Federal Reserve System. The New York Fed is the largest Reserve Bank in assets and volume of activity.

In Britain, gilt-edged market makers (GEMMS) are the dealers in gilts (short for gilt-edged securities because their edges were once gilded with gold leaf). Gilts are risk-free government bonds, similar to U.S. Treasuries. GEMMs work with InterDealer Brokers (IDBs) who provide a bridge to other market-makers. IDBs earn commissions by arranging transactions between GEMMs.

In Hong Kong, the Hong Kong Monetary Authority (the territory's de facto central bank) issues government-debt securities in the form of Exchange Fund notes and bills. The Exchange Fund represents Hong Kong's official reserves. Primary-market intermediaries are financial institutions appointed by the Hong Kong Monetary Authority.

In Japan, JGB (Japan Government Bond) Special Participants play a key primary market role in bidding on, purchasing, and underwriting specific shares of planned bond issues, with banks and other private financial institutions functioning as intermediaries.

THE PRIMARY MARKET

When an organization decides to issue a bond, the first step in the process is to contact an underwriter (normally an investment bank) to arrange the sale. The issuer takes into consideration the underwriter's experience and expertise before making its selection. More than 50 percent of all primary-market bond issues go to the top 10 names in what are known as the league tables, which rate investment banks on the size of their deals. Such names as J.P. Morgan and Goldman Sachs are often seen on the list of top underwriters for stocks and bonds based on their volume and fees.

The underwriter is responsible for advising an issuer on the timing of the sale as well as the terms of the offering, such as the interest rate and the size of the issue. The underwriter receives a fee for the services it provides, based on the issue size, market conditions, difficulty of selling the issue, and other variables.

Pricing the issue correctly is a critical factor in how well a bond issue will sell. Naturally, underwriters hope that interest rates do not rise before they sell the bonds. If they do, the price of the bonds may need to be reduced to make them more attractive to investors. Knowing the major purchasers of bonds is essential for underwriters since they could be stuck with bonds if they are unable to sell them. One important aspect and part of the selling process is to obtain a rating from a rating agency giving a stamp of approval on the issue. Favorable ratings are eagerly sought after by underwriters to make the bond more appealing. In fact, for some bond buyers a rating is required before a purchase is made (see Chapter 3). In some cases governments and other organizations could be given a rating covering all the debt instruments they issue, but today specific issues are rated when bonds possess unique characteristics.

To help market the bonds to investors and reduce their risk, underwriters often organize a syndicate of other underwriters. In a large issue, sharing the risk makes sense since no single underwriter alone would be able to cope with the financial burden of a failed bond sale. The underwriting managers or comanagers assume the most market risk until the bonds are sold. They allocate the bonds to other syndicate members, who sell the issue to institutions such as insurance companies and pension funds.

Underwriting serves the function of ensuring that bond issuers get their funds. If for some reason, such as a rise in interest rates, part of an issue fails to sell, the underwriter is obliged to cover any shortfall by paying the issuer the necessary amount.

BOND ISSUING PROCEDURES

At the start of the underwriting process the lead manager must send out an *invitation to underwrite* with a summary of the bond issue to potential co-managers in cases where a co-manager is required. This is followed by the prospectus or offering circular, which gives a comprehensive description of the bond issue and also includes detailed financial information about the issuer. An audit report prepared by auditors or accountants is included in the prospectus, and a selling group agreement between the lead manager and others in the syndicate is drawn up and signed.

Before the bond issue is officially announced in the financial press, a *gray* or unofficial market of banks that are not part of the underwriting syndicate is formed where preliminary assessment or *dealing* in the issue begins and potential investors are given the opportunity to size up the deal.

To publicize the upcoming issue, the selling syndicate takes out a newspaper notice known as a *tombstone*. This lists all the details of the issue and gives information about the issuer, the investment firms in the syndicate, and the auditors or accountants. One reason for giving a formal notice is to test the market to see if the bonds have been priced correctly. Bond prices have some room for maneuver during the selling period, although it's in the lead manager's best interest to keep the prices at or close to the issue price. However, if dealing on the gray market leads to lower prices, the lead manager might have to step in and buy up some of the bonds to keep prices stable.

There are three types of bond ownership forms: (1) bearer bonds, (2) registered bonds, and (3) book entry bonds.

Bearer Bonds

The name *bearer bond* describes the fact that whoever holds or *bears* the bond is the owner, and the bond issuer has no control over how the bond ownership can be transferred since no record is kept as to who owns the bonds. Normally, these bonds are issued in a fancy engraved certificate on high quality paper with all kinds of security characteristics to prevent fraud because, in effect, they are like currency. Whoever produces the certificate can trade such bonds. In order to collect interest, the certificate has a series of coupons attached, which can be remitted for interest payments so that when an interest payment is due the bond owner clips the coupon and produces it for payment. The problem with bearer bonds is that if they are lost or stolen then the rightful owner has lost out. This is why they are attractive to robbers or people who want to launder or transfer large amounts of money without leaving a record or paper trail. Because of this, bearer bonds are becoming less common, although Eurobonds are still issued in bearer form.

Registered Bonds

Like bearer bonds, registered bonds are also issued in printed engraved certificates, but unlike bearer bonds, the issuer maintains a record of who owns each bond with the owner's name and address printed on the certificate. If the owner sells the bond and needs to transfer, he must endorse the certificate by signing it and presenting it to the issuer's transfer agent. Then the transfer agent cancels the certificate and issues a new certificate to the new owner. The issuer thus will always know who owns the bonds and is able to make interest payments without going through the inconvenience of receiving actual coupons. The problem with registered bonds it that it takes time for transfer agents to issue new certificates, and trading in the bond can't proceed without that process being completed.

Book Entry Bonds

In the case of book entry bonds ownership is recorded electronically by a central depository or central register. Sometimes a master certificate is held for the entire bond issuance, although this is not really needed. Whenever a bond is sold, the transfer from the old owner to the new owner is made by the depository on its computer records, and a receipt for the transaction is made. In order to facilitate trading, the depository listed brokers and dealers as the owners instead of their clients, the actual owners. Then, the broker or dealer maintains its own records of the actual or beneficial owners. If a broker executes a trade between two of its own clients, it is not necessary to inform the depository of the transaction, since the broker is shown as the owner in the depository's records.

THE SECONDARY MARKET

Once a bond has been issued in the primary market, it can be traded in the secondary market, such as the one operated by the NYSE. Most trading activity, however, occurs electronically via computers and telephones

NOTE
CUSTODIAN BANK

MARKET MAKERS

Market makers are what the name implies, they *make* markets or create markets by becoming both a buyer and seller. The market maker can be an individual or a company. He gives offers to both buyers and sellers, and makes a *spread* between the buy and sell price. Market makers can be found in foreign exchange markets, commodity markets, stock markets, and bond markets. In the foreign exchange area, banks normally play the market maker role. In stock exchanges, the market makers are both individuals and brokers. For example on some stock exchanges there are market makers known as *specialists*, who act as the official market maker for a specific security so that they become the experts in that security, taking positions on both the buy and sell side, and taking the responsibility for ensuring an orderly market with less volatility. In essence, market makers earn by buying a bond at a lower price than the price at which they sell or sell a stock at a higher price than what they purchased. The idea is to make money in both rising and falling market by taking advantage of the difference between the *bid* and *offer* prices.

CUSTODIANS

Security custodians are normally banks. They are responsible for safekeeping financial assets such as bonds and stocks. Sometimes, they are specialized in only the safekeeping role, but more often today they are part of a large diversified bank. Custodians not only safekeep various types of securities as well as precious metals and cash currency, but also arrange for securities settlements of sales and purchases; collect bond interest payments or stock dividend payments; make deliveries of securities; make tax payments and records; take care of various corporate actions such as bond interest payments and stock dividends; provide information regarding company meetings or bond holder meetings; act on behalf of clients at such meetings; and many other activities related to security transactions. Custodian banks are often global in their operations with local branches undertaking the custodial function. They also contract other local custodian banks to work on their behalf.

TRANSFER AGENTS

Transfer agents act on behalf of stock and bond issuers to keep a record of the individuals and entities that own their stocks and bonds. As in the case of custodians, most transfer agents are banks or trust

(*continued*)

(*Continued*)

companies, although there are some companies that act as their own transfer agent. The main tasks of a transfer agent are to (1) issue or cancel stock or bond ownership records, so that there is an accurate record of ownership, (2) keep records of who owns the company's stocks and bonds and how many shares or bonds each investor owns, (3) act as a middleman for the company or entity issuing the stocks or bonds by acting as the paying agent to pay bond interest or stock dividends and other payments, (4) distribute company reports and bond documents, (5) help bond or stock owners with such matters as lost or stolen records of ownership.

through a network of dealers. In the secondary market, investors purchase existing bonds from other investors, rather than from the issuer. Most bonds are traded by investment banks, which are market makers for specific debt issues. Investors who want to buy or sell a bond must call the bank that makes a market in that bond and ask for a price quotation.

While many buyers prefer to hold their bonds until the maturity date, some may want or need to sell before then. The buy-and-hold strategy can lead to illiquidity in some secondary markets with little trading taking place. Many bonds are held to maturity; nevertheless, the secondary market for Eurobonds, as well as for U.S. Treasury notes, bills, and bonds, is enormous. Daily trading volume of the U.S. government bonds alone can be in excess of US$500 billion.

There are plenty of reasons why there is a secondary market for bonds and why all investors do not keep their bonds until maturity. These reasons include:

1. To take advantage of yield differences. For example, if an investor has a low-rated bond and finds that a higher-rated bond is priced close to the low-rated bond, he might sell the low-rated bond and buy the higher-rated one to take advantage or the low spread in prices with the expectation that the higher-rated bond will trade at a higher price in the future.

2. Credit-upside trade. When an investor buys a bond expecting credit upgrade from a rating agency.

3. Credit defense trade. When an investor sells a bond expecting credit downgrade from a rating agency.

4. New issues swaps. When an investor buys bonds currently being issued and sells the older bonds in order to obtain higher liquidity.

5. Sector-rotation trades. To move from one industry sector to another, which is expected to perform better.

6. Yield-curve adjustment trades. In cases where the long-term interest rate is expected to rise and short-term interest rate decrease (or rise less), an investor may want to sell the long-term bonds and buy the short-term bonds.

7. Structure trades. Moving from one type of bond to another such as selling a callable bond and buying a non-callable bond.

In their forays into the secondary market, bond investors may encounter a variety of individuals. These include:

Brokers: Third parties who buy and sell bonds for an investor. They earn their commissions by raising the price when the investor buys and lowering it at the time of sale. They do not take possession of the bond for resale.

Dealers/traders: Individuals or firms that act as a principal or market maker in a securities transaction. They hold the bonds on their books and trade for their own account, aiming to profit from reselling.

InterDealer brokers: A brokerage firm that serves as an intermediary between major dealers or a member of the London Stock Exchange who only deals with market-makers and not the general public.

Sales staff: People who provide investors, or clients, with information about the market and bond prices, and who refer transaction orders to traders. Salespeople maintain contact with all categories of players.

Economists/analysts: Experts who gather and analyze information about the marketplace and prepare market forecasts for the financial industry to use for investment guidance.

THE REPO MARKET

Repo is an abbreviation for *repossession.* The repo rate is the discount rate that a central bank uses to repurchase government securities from commercial banks. This depends on the level of money supply the central bank wants to maintain in the country. Therefore, to temporarily expand money supply the central bank decreases the repo rate. The banks can then swap their government bond holdings for cash. In order to reduce the money supply, the central bank increases the repo rate.

Repos refer to repurchase agreements, or contracts, that involve selling and buying back a bond or other financial assets at an agreed price and at a future date. In other words, the seller is temporarily selling a financial asset in order to obtain a short-term loan, with the securities pledged as collateral with the understanding that he must purchase the asset back in the future.

The difference between what the assets are sold for and what it costs to buy it back represents the interest gain, or repo rate, for the purchasing party when he returns the asset to the original seller. The repo rate is negotiated between buyer and seller and represents the cost of the loan. Since the "loan" is secured with the bond asset, the interest rate, not unexpectedly, is usually lower than that asked by a bank for an unsecured loan.

A reverse repurchase agreement (reverse repo) is the other side of the coin, with a seller agreeing to buy the instrument and reselling it back to the buyer at an agreed price and at an agreed future date.

Repo transactions are normally conducted by institutions, professional investors, and high-net-worth individuals, since most involve large amounts of money. Central banks often use repos as a form of monetary control by adding or draining cash from money markets.

The size of the repo market is very large. The average daily amount outstanding of the repo market for U.S. government securities is in excess of US$3 trillion.

NOTE
TRANSPARENCY IN THE BOND MARKET: TRACE

Transparency is an issue of genuine concern in the bond market. The lack of centralized reporting of transactions and private negotiations conducted between buyers and sellers has made it difficult to get up-to-the-minute prices on individual bonds, especially for smaller issues. In the United States a new system called the Transaction Report and Compliance Engine (TRACE) was introduced in 2002. The system allows public dissemination of real-time transaction and price data on U.S. corporate-bond trading in the secondary market. The system covers over 20,000 corporate bonds and over 90 percent of the trading. Sale prices must be reported within 15 minutes of the trade and can be used by investors to confirm that they are paying a fair market price for their bonds. It also shows how much of a markup the broker is charging to sell that bond and enables yield comparisons to be made against those of comparable bonds.

BONDS AND ECONOMICS

Many economic factors can affect the bond market and cause swings in bond prices. Interest rates, of course, are a key factor, but not the only one. Expectations are what drive prices, as well as what is actually happening. As indicated earlier, a rise in interest rates causes bond prices to fall. Falling interest rates push bond prices up.

If the economy is racing along too fast, higher interest rates are often used by governments and central banks to apply the brakes on the economy. This may be good news for those who plan to buy and hold new bonds offering those higher rates, but not for those holding bonds bound at lower interest rates. Falling prices for bonds paying lower rates are a downside of rising interest rates.

When an economy starts sliding into recession, central banks and government try to engineer interest rate declines to encourage more borrowing and stimulate the economy. This is good for holders of existing bonds that are yielding the higher rate, but not for those who bought bonds at the new lower rate. The upside of a shift to lower rates is thus higher bond prices for those holding bonds paying the old, higher interest rates.

Organizations and factors impacting bond prices include central banks, currency movements, economic growth, inflation, the balance of trade, consumer behavior, changes in regulations, and how those regulations are interpreted and applied. We describe some of these factors below, but it is important to keep in mind that there are so many factors interacting with each other that simple correlations and conclusions cannot be easily drawn, and thus data should be used with caution.

Central Banks

In the United States the Federal Reserve (the Fed) is the central bank. It controls monetary policy and has the power to raise or lower interest rates to keep inflation at bay and boost economic growth. Investors typically await the Fed's decisions on interest rates and money supply in order to obtain an insight regarding bond prices.

If interest rates are lowered, businesses and consumers can borrow money more easily, and the pace of the economy picks up, although a consequence may be inflation. High interest rates, on the other hand, discourage borrowing, and the economy slows down, along with inflation. As the U.S. central bank, the Fed has some important powers that enable it to impact interest rates and expand or contract the country's money supply in order to impact the economy's growth rate.

Open-Market Operations

By buying or selling U.S. Treasuries or federal agency bonds, the Fed can add or remove money from the system. This affects the *federal funds rate*, the rate at which banks borrow reserves from one another overnight. When the Fed buys bonds and pays for them in cash, money is put back into the system, which leads to lower interest rates and stimulates the economy. When the Fed sells bonds, it takes in money for those bonds and money supply gets tighter so that interest rates rise and inflation should ease. Of course, the impact of the Fed's actions is not always so direct because of so many other factors impacting interest rates, inflation, and economic growth.

The Fed can also change the *discount rate* or the rate at which banks pay to borrow from the government. A small change in the rate in terms of basis points (100 basis points equals to 1 percent) has a knock-on impact on what rates banks lend to customers. If the banks pay higher rates to borrow, this tends to be passed on to their customers. Higher rates have the effect of slowing the economy.

The Fed can also impact interest rates by changing the *reserve requirements*—the requirement banks have to hold money in reserve as a percentage of their outstanding loans or deposit liabilities. A higher reserve amount means that the bank must keep more money with the Fed and thus has less money to lend. This, of course, can cause the cost of money, the interest rates, to rise.

Currencies

A strong currency can affect the bond market positively or negatively. For example, the U.S. dollar strengthens when more people around the world want dollars rather than other currencies. This, of course, makes dollar-denominated bonds more attractive and can lead to changes in U.S. dollar interest rates. During times of international crisis, investors have tended to flock to the safe havens of gold, the U.S. dollar, and U.S. Treasuries. This predictable psychological behavior can create a demand for U.S. dollars and bonds, resulting in interest rate changes.

Economic Growth

The best single snapshot of the size of a country's domestic economy is its gross domestic product (GDP). GDP measures the market value of all goods and services produced by a country over a given period, usually a calendar year. Generally, the lower the GDP, the more bullish the market for trading bonds. High GDP growth figures tend to cause bond yields to soar and the prices of existing bonds, which do not have such high rates, to fall. Therefore economic growth characteristics of the country are a factor to consider when estimating the direction of bond prices.

Inflation

Inflation and interest rates are inextricably intertwined and a critical factor for investors. If, for example, inflation is running at 5 percent per year, a US$1 today will be worth only 95 cents a year from now, since inflation would have wiped out the buying power of the dollar by 5 percent.

If investors are to obtain a real return on their money, they need to know that they can earn more than the annual inflation rate. In the United States and other countries, there are a number of indicators that enable investors to evaluate the inflationary outlook, such as the wholesale or producers price index, which measures the average monthly change in wholesale prices (an early indicator of inflation); the consumer price index, which measures the changes in prices of a fixed basket of products and services; and commodity indices such as the Commodity Research Bureau's Index, which tracks the prices of a basket of commodities.

Employment

Rising unemployment could be a signal for a slowing of the economy and thus for lower interest rates and higher bond prices. Conversely, lower unemployment could indicate that the economy is heating up and thus be a signal for higher interest rates and lower bond prices. Employment data just like other data can be skewed by such factors as seasonal layoffs or unexpected weather conditions, and must be used judiciously. An increase in those registering as unemployed makes the bond market bullish because it suggests the economy is slowing down and that central banks could opt for lower interest rates to stimulate the economy and thus cause old bonds with high interest rates to rise.

In addition to pure employment numbers, the number of hours worked, how much people are paid, increases in overtime, and higher average hourly earnings are all indicators to watch.

Trade Balance

The *balance of trade* refers to a nation's imports vis-à-vis its exports. Many factors can influence a country's balance of trade, such as exchange-rate movements, production costs, raw material costs, taxes, and trade restrictions. In the United States, for example, a strong dollar hurts exports because it makes U.S. products more expensive relative to other currencies. In this situation, imports increase because U.S. dollars can buy more for less. A weak dollar makes U.S. goods cheaper for others to purchase, so U.S. exports rise and imports of now costlier foreign-made products fall. A strong dollar relative to other currencies makes exports more expensive and imports cheaper, thus resulting in more imports than exports and a negative trade balance. A weak currency could cause investors to retreat from bonds denominated in that currency and cause interest rates to rise, since countries and companies attempting to raise loans will find it more difficult to attract buyers.

Consumer Behavior

Free-spending, optimistic consumers tend to cause the bond market to turn bearish because of inflation fears. Consumer pessimism tends to work in favor of the bond market, since the economy downshifts when people spend less. For the same reason, a fall in the consumer savings rate could be bullish for bonds. But, paradoxically, if the savings rate increases dramatically, the bond market might also be happy because this could be interpreted as meaning more money is available to buy bonds.

Other Factors

Financial professionals and investors pore over many other indicators in their quest to discover future economic trends and how these might influence the bond market. These include:

- Corporate profits (usually good for most bonds if they go down, bad if they go up)
- Durable-goods orders (a decrease is a sign that the economy is heading in the same direction, which could be good for bonds; the opposite would be true if orders are going up)
- Housing starts (an upswing means the economy and interest rates are bouncing back)
- New home sales (the longer it takes to sell homes, the worse the economy, which tend to favor bonds)
- Retail sales (a spike in retail sales indicates a strong economy, which is bad for bonds)

Regulatory Bodies

Governments around the world make serious efforts to regulate their securities markets to protect investors. Central banks such as the U.S. Federal Reserve and the Bank of England oversee the primary markets, while government agencies, including the Securities and Exchange Commission (SEC) in the United States and the Financial Services Authority in Britain, deal with issues that affect the secondary market.

Stock exchanges impose their own rules and regulations on members' actions. The National Association of Securities Dealers (NASD), which reports to the SEC, monitors the NASDAQ, the largest U.S. electronic market.

The International Capital Market Association (ICMA) provides a self-regulatory framework of rules governing ethical and standardized trading practices in international bond markets, as well as bond-market transparency.

The Securities Industry and Financial Markets Association (SIFMA) is an international voice dedicated to strengthening capital markets and supporting investors. With offices in New York, Washington, DC, London, and

Hong Kong, it represents more than 650 member firms in the United States and around the world.

These and many other regulatory bodies have an impact on bond markets and bond prices through changes in regulations and how those regulations are interpreted and applied.

SUMMARY

Bond markets are one of three legs of what are collectively known as the world's capital markets—the other two being money markets and equity markets. Unlike equity markets, which often have physical exchanges for buying and selling, most bond trading takes place electronically on the over-the-counter market.

Bonds are initially issued by a government, corporation, or financial institution on the primary market, usually through an investment bank. Bonds may also be traded on the secondary market, although many bond investors choose to hold their bonds until maturity.

A variety of economic factors can affect bond markets and bond prices. Interest-rate actions by the U.S. Federal Reserve Board have the single greatest impact. The value of the U.S. dollar, gross domestic product, inflation, employment, the balance of trade, consumer behavior, and other indicators are also weighed by bond investors.

QUICK QUIZ

1. Give two reasons why the bond market often operates as an over-the-counter entity rather than through established exchanges.
2. Describe the three categories of market players in the bond market.
3. Explain the steps involved in issuing a bond on the primary market.
4. What are some of the economic factors that can affect bond values, and why do they have such an effect?
5. Explain what TRACE is and how it has improved transparency in the bond market.

3 RATING AGENCIES

Before buying a bond, an investor naturally wants to confirm that the bond principal and interest will be paid, and thus he must know how creditworthy the issuer is. Research is thus necessary to delve into the history, track record, and financial strength of the borrower. Of course, this is time consuming and requires experts in various industries. For this reason rating agencies developed. Soon their extensive research became well known and appreciated by investors to the extent that institutional bond investors came to depend on their ratings and were even required by their directors to obtain those ratings.

The bond credit ratings enable investors to tell at a glance how risky or how safe a bond is by checking the bond's rating. Of course, that is not to say that rating agencies don't make mistakes in noticing possible financial risks in the firms being assessed. Higher-rated bonds pay lower rates of interest because they are perceived to be safer. A lower-rated bond is riskier and typically offers a higher rate of interest to compensate for the greater risk. A bond's rating can also affect its market price after the initial issue.

Armed with ratings, an investor can design a bond portfolio to take advantage of higher interest rates (at higher risk) or opt for a more conservative position by choosing bonds with lower rates, but that provide a safer return on investment. Certain bonds, such as U.S. government obligations, are not rated because they are considered to be risk-free, meaning there is virtually no chance of default. After all, the government can always resort to printing more money should it ever come to that. When commenting on the safety of government bond investments, one famous chief of Citibank once said: "Governments never fail." However, experience has shown that governments do fail, and government bonds often end up worthless.

For example, bond holders around the world invested heavily in Chinese government bonds issued before the People's Republic of China (PRC) was established in 1949. The PRC subsequently defaulted on these loans. In many cases, the bonds were handed down to the grandchildren of the original bondholders in hopes of repayment. The American Bondholders Foundation continued the fight to get those bonds paid.

Similarly, the Russian government defaulted on US$40 billion worth of bonds in 1998. Speculative attacks on the ruble and concerns about the country's economic stability led to the defaults. Argentina defaulted on US$90 billion in debt obligations in 2001, repaying only 25 cents on the dollar. The country was denounced by creditors worldwide and was still struggling to pay off its debts years later. There are other examples of defaults in recent history: One of them is the default of Icelandic banks in 2008. Completely privatized in 2003, the Icelandic banking sector relied on the availability of ample foreign wholesale funding to rapidly expand abroad and accumulate almost 900 percent of GDP in assets by the end of 2007. At the same time, gross external indebtedness reached 550 percent of GDP at the end of 2007, largely on account of the banks. The loss of confidence in Iceland's financial system in October 2008 led to the collapse of its three largest banks in the span of a week.

Greece without the joint euro area/IMF financing package of €110 billion granted in May 2010 would have defaulted on its sovereign debt.

Within the vast universe of corporate bonds and exotic debt instruments from around the world, risk does apply, and thus credit rating agencies play an important role.

CREDIT-RATING AGENCIES

Rating agencies in the United States and internationally attempt to separate the wheat from the chaff by distinguishing between investment-grade and non–investment-grade issues and by assigning letter designations that indicate the quality of bond issues. For example, a triple A (AAA) rating may be an agency's top investment-grade rating, while a D might signal a company in default. Although rating agencies may each use slightly different scales (Moody's top grade is Aaa; Standard & Poor's is AAA), comparing the various systems is relatively easy.

An investment-grade debt instrument is considered safer and less likely to default than a non–investment-grade (speculative) security. The latter are sometimes referred to as *junk bonds* or *high-yield bonds.*

Before a letter-based rating is assigned, rating agencies dispatch analysts to interview executives about their organization's operations and to pore over the organization's financial data. They look at the amount of an issuer's outstanding debt, its balance sheet, projected revenue growth, and other data.

Worldwide, dozens of credit-rating agencies ply their trade analyzing the creditworthiness of corporations and public entities that issue debt, but three U.S.-based agencies effectively dominate the US$5-billion-a year-industry—Moody's, Standard & Poor's, and Fitch Ratings.

HISTORICAL BACKGROUND

Agencies such as Moody's, Standard & Poor's, Fitch, and A. M. Best have histories dating back a century or more. In 1936, in the midst of the Great Depression, the modern era of the rating industry began when the U.S.

government declared that banks had to limit themselves to investment-grade securities. Over time, the introduction of a host of regulatory requirements meant that not only banks, but insurers, mutual funds, and other financial institutions had to take note of bond ratings.

The opinions of these agencies are enormously influential, and ratings are closely monitored by investors and other market participants. This is particularly true given the global growth of financial markets and the introduction of complex financial products, such as asset-backed securities and derivatives. Major agencies in the United States are also finding new opportunities to extend their reach overseas as financial markets become increasingly globalized.

Credit ratings can have an influence on how hard or easy it is for an issuer to gain access to capital, how much interest is paid on a bond, and even whether certain investments are undertaken. The lower the rating, the harder it is for an issuer to borrow money, and the higher the interest rate that has to be paid. That's why corporate junk bonds generally pay higher yields than investment-grade debt. They can be profitable, but the risk is higher.

Regulators, such as the SEC, use credit ratings as a way of keeping track of the investment risks from financial products issued by corporations and organizations within their jurisdiction. Besides serving as a handy guide for gauging risk levels, ratings are used in many other ways as a benchmark for legislation, regulations, and in private financial contracts.

NRSRO

The SEC adopted the term Nationally Recognized Statistical Rating Organization (NRSRO) in 1975 in connection with a requirement relating to debt securities held by broker-dealers. If the rating agency that issued an investment grade rating for these securities was "nationally recognized," then lower safety margins against losses arising from market fluctuations in the broker-dealers' positions would be allowed.

The criteria used to decide whether to grant NRSRO status to a credit-rating agency included reviews of its organizational structure, its financial resources, the size and quality of its staff, and its independence from the entities it rated.

Ten rating agencies overseen by the U.S. Securities and Exchange Commission (SEC) were assigned NRSRO status, which means that their ratings are considered credible measures of creditworthiness for regulatory purposes. They include:

1. Moody's Investors Service, Inc.

2. Standard and Poor's Ratings Services

3. Fitch Ratings

4. A. M. Best Company, Inc.
5. DBRS, Ltd
6. Japan Credit Rating Agency, Ltd
7. Rating and Investment Information, Inc.
8. Egan-Jones Rating Co
9. LACE Financial Corporation
10. Realpoint LLC.

Formerly, a credit-rating agency would gain NRSRO recognition via what was called a "No Action Letter" from the SEC. After undertaking the necessary research, the SEC would issue such a letter as a way of saying that it wouldn't recommend any enforcement action against the broker/dealers who relied on ratings issued by the NRSRO.

Criticism arose over the "No Action Letter" policy, with claims that the approach was not transparent enough and that it gave the SEC too little regulatory oversight. Fallout from the Enron and WorldCom financial scandals in 2002 and the failure of the leading credit-rating agencies to detect

NEWS CLIP
RATING AGENCIES GO ON STRIKE

In 2010, some rating agencies refused to allow their ratings to be included in initial public offerings of bonds and stocks prospectuses and other offering documents for fear of being sued for false or misleading information. The rating agencies embarked on a seller's strike because of the increased liability mandated by new financial reform legislation that gave ratings agencies "expert status," making them as liable as the underwriters of a security issue. The legislation repealed Rule 436(g) under Section 11 of the 1933 Act, which exempted NRSROs from expert status. Expert status takes away the common law protections that ratings agencies had. The agencies were concerned not only by the reduced levels of legal protection but also by the higher levels of liability. This is expected to result in higher fee levels charged by the ratings agencies to compensate for the higher potential liability.

serious problems at both companies also helped drive calls for an overhaul of the system. This came with the passage of the Credit Rating Agency Reform Act in 2006, which introduced more stringent SEC measures. The Act gave the SEC rulemaking authority over recordkeeping, financial reports, procedures for handling nonpublic information, conflicts of interest that must be avoided, and practices that an NRSRO must not engage in.

WHO USES RATING AGENCIES?

Individual investors rely heavily on credit ratings, but so do many other market participants. Issuers, for example, desire a positive rating in order to borrow on better terms or to market their debt obligations to investors more easily. A good rating is also regarded as an affirmation of the issuer's belief in its own creditworthiness. Some companies may want a rating to see how their management and corporate performance are measuring up.

Mutual funds, pension funds, and insurance companies are among the largest buyers of debt securities in the United States. Although institutional investors typically perform their own in-house credit analyses to meet in-house risk-management criteria, they use credit ratings to find out what outside analysts think of a particular issue or to anticipate what might happen with a credit rating in the future. They may also need ratings to comply with regulatory requirements and with internal policies that specify certain minimum ratings for investments.

Broker-dealers who sell debt securities have a vested interest in credit ratings, too. Like institutional buyers, they conduct their own financial investigations and often use credit ratings to double-check their own conclusions. One important difference between them is that many broker-dealers have ratings advisory groups that help underwriting clients choose credit-rating agencies and that shepherd them through the rating process.

Financial authorities around the world use credit ratings for regulatory purposes. Banking regulators allow banks to use credit ratings from certain rating agencies when calculating their net-capital-reserve requirements. Another use of credit ratings is in private contracts where cash collateral or repayment of outstanding loans can be demanded if a credit rating slips below a certain level.

Many individual and institutional investors will accept nothing less than a *bona fide* NRSRO when seeking a credit rating. Some, in fact, want ratings from at least three reputable agencies. Whether this gives the big players a competitive advantage is a question that has been asked many times and continues to be debated. Others feel that with 10 rating agencies currently anointed as NRSROs, enough competition already exists.

CONFLICTS OF INTEREST

Critics charge that conflict of interest is an issue because the larger credit-reporting agencies earn their revenue from the issuers of bonds that they rate. The agencies' response is that widespread public availability of ratings makes the issuer-pays model the most appropriate way for them to do business. However, some smaller agencies have resorted to a subscription-based model, which, they contend, reduces the potential for conflicts of interest.

Egan-Jones, for example, has operated on a subscription basis since the company was founded in 1995. Its more than 500 institutional subscribers pay anything from US$25,000 to US$280,000 in annual subscriptions for access to the company's ratings and reports. Each client is charged according to the amount of service required. The company is expected to offer its services to retail investors in the near future.

Other criticism has been leveled at agencies for failing to lower their ratings quickly enough when a company is in trouble. Enron, for instance, kept its investment-grade rating until four days before filing for bankruptcy on December 2, 2001.

Scrutinized for their role in the wave of corporate accounting scandals earlier in the decade, credit-rating agencies came under fire again in 2007 and 2008: U.S. Congressional hearings were held on the impact that conflicts of interests may have had on the subprime credit crisis, particularly with regard to the ratings for mortgage-backed securities.

Dissatisfaction with the agencies' efforts at self-regulation led to the credit-rating industry being put under SEC oversight in 2007. In the wake of the subprime crisis, the SEC adopted new rules in December 2008 to address conflicts of interest as well as improve transparency and accountability at credit-rating agencies. Critics say the rules still don't go far enough. In 2010, the agencies' role in the crisis was being probed by the Senate's Permanent Subcommittee on Investigations.

Despite their history, the agencies have managed to retain their clout, and investors and the business community continue to rely on them.

RATING AGENCY PROFILES

Moody's

Credit ratings began their rapid development in 1909 when 41-year-old John Moody published his Moody's Analyses of Railroad Investments, which assigned stock and bond ratings using letter grades. Moody had started out in the field of finance almost two decades earlier, working as an errand boy at a Wall Street bank for US$20 a week.

A strong entrepreneurial spirit carried Moody through the ups and downs of the stock market in the early twentieth century. In 1913, he branched out into rating industrial companies and utilities. Moody's Investors Services was officially born in New York on July 1, 1914. In 1917, Moody's fledgling company began expanding into rating bonds issued by the U.S. government and municipalities. Ten years later, the company's ratings covered nearly all of the U.S. bond market. When default rates rose during the Great Depression, most of the bonds that Moody's rated highly were still meeting their financial obligations. By 1970, Moody's ratings were also being used for grading commercial paper and bank deposits.

Today, the company's ratings are carried on "any type of debt or obligation of interest to institutional investors," including bonds, debentures, asset-backed and mortgage-backed securities, convertible bonds, medium-term notes, derivative securities, and so on. Moody's currently maintains a presence in 28 countries and serves markets in more than 100 countries around the world.

Moody's embraces a multidisciplinary or "universal" approach to risk analysis that involves assessing and understanding a variety of relevant factors and viewpoints. The process of assigning a rating starts with gathering information from publicly available data—annual reports, prospectuses, offering circulars, offering memoranda, trust deeds, and indentures of particular securities. Other useful information may include market data, such as stock price trends, trading volume, and bond spread.

The company's analysts scour economic data from industry groups, agencies, and bodies such as the World Bank. Further information is gleaned from books and articles drawn from financial, academic, and news sources, with experts in industry, government, or academia also consulted.

Once a conclusion is reached, the lead analyst for the issuer, industry, country, or asset type under study submits recommendations to a rating committee that may vary in size depending on such things as the complexity of the security, the issuer's size, or the nature of the transaction. The committee's discussions are strictly confidential. After a rating has been assigned, Moody's continues to monitor the company or security to determine if circumstances require any changes. The marketplace is informed about any further actions that Moody's might take.

Moody's ratings rank an issuer's general long-term creditworthiness or the credit quality of individual obligations against expected loss. The latter is defined as (a) the probability of default and (b) the financial loss suffered in the event of a default. The general expectation is that lower-rated issuers and debts will, on average, default more frequently than those that are more highly rated. The current market price of an issue has no relation to its rating.

Moody's rating scale runs from a high of Aaa—representing the minimum credit risk—to a low of C, assigned to bonds that are typically in default, with little chance of interest or principal being recovered. The lowest investment-grade rating is Baa3.

The scale for long-term debt (maturities of one year or more) contains a total of 21 generic letter grades and is divided into two classifications—investment and speculative grades. Each letter-grade category features accompanying numerical symbols, such as 1, 2, or 3, which are used to further refine the rating grade.

Historically, the default rate for Aaa securities is insignificant, although as one moves farther down the scale, the risk of default rises. For short-term debt (maturities of less than one year), four grades are assigned—Prime-1 (the highest ability to repay short-term debt) is followed by Prime-2, Prime-3, and Not Prime.

Rating outlooks, which indicate the likely direction a rating might take over the medium term, are also given and fall into four categories: positive, negative, stable, and developing. Ratings may be obtained on the company's website (www.moodys.com).

If no rating is assigned or if one has been withdrawn, this doesn't necessarily mean that questions are being raised about the issue's creditworthiness. If there is no rating, it could be that an application wasn't received, data about the issue or the issuer was missing, the issue was being privately placed—in which case a rating wouldn't be published—or that Moody's doesn't rate the issue or issuer as a matter of company policy. A rating might be withdrawn if, for example, new circumstances came up that effectively precluded re-analysis of the issue, if up-to-date data weren't available for a revised judgment, or if the bond was redeemed.

If a rating is under review for an upgrade/downgrade or if uncertainty exists about the direction the rating will take, the security is placed on a watch list. In general, such a review is completed in 90 days. Moody's may change the rating of an issue at any time should the financial situation of the issuer or the debt obligation warrant it. This is more likely to occur among lower-rated bonds.

MOODY'S RATINGS SCALE

Long-term debt ratings (maturities of one year or more)

Aaa	Highest rating, representing minimum credit risk
Aa1, Aa2, Aa3	High grade
A1, A2, A3	Upper-medium grade
Baa1, Baa2, Baa3	Medium grade
Ba1, Ba2, Ba3	Speculative elements
B1, B2, B3	Subject to high credit risk
Caa1, Caa2, Caa3	Bonds of poor standing
Ca	Highly speculative, or near default
C	Lowest rating, bonds typically in default, little prospect for recovery of principal or interest

Short-term debt ratings (maturities of less than one year)

Prime-1	Highest ability to repay debt
Prime-2	High ability to repay debt
Prime-3	Acceptable ability to repay debt
Not Prime	Not rated as any of the Prime rankings

Fitch Ratings

Founded in New York City by John Knowles Fitch in 1913, the Fitch Publishing Company started out as a publisher of financial statistics. It soon began addressing the investment community's needs with publications such as the *Fitch Bond Book* and the *Fitch Stock and Bond Manual.*

In 1924, the company began in-depth analyses of financial securities and introduced its ratings scale, featuring letter grades from AAA to D. The agency began to grow dramatically in the 1990s. In 1997, the company merged with London-based IBCA Ltd, increasing Fitch's worldwide presence. The merger also brought Fitch under the ownership of IBCA's holding company, Fimilac S.A.

Three years later, Fitch acquired Duff & Phelps Credit Rating Co., based in Chicago, and the rating business of Thomson BankWatch. These acquisitions helped it broaden its coverage in the corporate, banking, financial institution, insurance, and structured finance sectors. It was subsequently renamed Fitch Ratings.

Today, the global rating agency, which is headquartered in New York and London, employs over 1,900 professional staff in 49 offices worldwide.

Fitch is best known for its credit ratings, but it also publishes a variety of other ratings, scores, and measures that assess an organization's financial or operational strength. It rates asset managers, managed funds, and servicers of residential and commercial mortgages, for example.

The credit ratings evaluate an organization's ability to meet its financial obligations; that is, its ability to make interest payments or repay the principal on a debt obligation. The ratings cover corporate, sovereign, financial, bank, insurance, municipal, and other public finance entities, plus structured finance securities and other obligations.

Fitch's ratings for investment-grade, long-term financial instruments (maturities of one year or more) with low to moderate credit risk range from AAA to BBB–; short-term instruments of similar quality are rated F1 to F3. Speculative or non–investment grade categories are rated BB+ to D for international long-term instruments and B to D for short-term ones. Long-term categories from AA to CCC may be further defined with plus or minus signs. The ranking for short-term debt may have a plus sign to denote exceptionally robust credit. Non-investment grades indicate a higher level of credit risk or actual default.

International credit ratings address an issuer's ability to meet its obligations in a foreign or local currency. For certain markets, Fitch also issues national ratings that assess credit quality in relation to a country's "best" credit risk. Instruments issued or guaranteed by the sovereign state are assigned the "best" rating.

Fitch bases its ratings on publicly available information and that sourced from the issuer and underwriters, along with reports filed with regulatory agencies, industry and economic data, and insights from analysts. The information is gathered through face-to-face meetings, site visits, teleconferences, and by other contacts.

Besides reviewing the available information, the primary analyst meets with top executives and management of the entity. Since the main consideration in assigning a rating is the entity's future prospects, medium-term projections of operating and financial information are a key element, because they point to whether the organization is likely to achieve its strategic goals.

The formal rating is assigned by a rating committee of at least four analysts, including the primary analyst. The issuer can request an appeal of the rating decision, which may be granted if relevant additional information is available. This review is normally completed within two business days.

If not enough information is available to determine the creditworthiness of an entity or a transaction, then no rating will be assigned. A "shadow" or conditional rating may be assigned in cases requiring an abbreviated analysis, if information is limited or if part of the analysis has been omitted. A shadow rating is designated by an asterisk after the letter grade—for example, BB*—and is generally not made available to the public.

A Rating Watch is assigned in cases where there is a "reasonable probability of a rating change"—positive, negative, or evolving (upgraded, downgraded, or maintained). A positive, negative, or stable Rating Outlook estimates in which direction a rating is likely to move over a one- to two-year time frame.

Ratings for new and existing entities are available at no charge on Fitch's public website (www.fitchratings.com) and released to major news agencies.

FITCH RATINGS' SCALE

Long-term credit ratings

AAA	Highest credit quality, lowest expectation of credit risk
AA	Very high credit quality
A	High credit quality
BBB	Good credit quality
BB	Speculative
B	Highly speculative
CCC	Default is a real possibility
CC	Default appears probable
C	Default is imminent
RD	Failure to make due payments on some but not all financial obligations
D	Default on all financial obligations

Short-term debt ratings (less than 13 months or up to 3 years for U.S. public finance issues)

F1	Highest credit quality
F2	Good credit quality
F3	Fair credit quality
B	Speculative
C	High default rate
D	Default

Standard & Poor's

Standard & Poor's history dates back to 1860 when Henry Varnum Poor published his *History of Railroads and Canals of the United States*, an exhaustive look at the financial and operational details of the U.S. railroad industry. In 1906, the Standard Statistics Bureau was formed by Luther Lee Blake. The company's main business was providing financial news items about U.S. corporations. Ten years later, it began grading bonds.

In 1941, Poor's Publishing merged with Standard Statistics to form the Standard & Poor's Corp. The Standard & Poor's Stock Index, a list of the stocks of 500 large-cap companies, was introduced in 1957. After the Dow Jones Industrial Average, the S&P 500 is the most closely followed indicator of large-cap stocks and also serves as a barometer of the broader U.S. economy.

Standard & Poor's products and services include credit ratings, equity research, risk evaluation, and data services. Acquired by the McGraw-Hill Companies, Inc. in 1966, the agency issues credit ratings for both public and private corporations. The ratings represent the agency's opinion of an issuer's creditworthiness or that of the debt security or financial obligation. The firm has approximately 8,500 employees in 23 countries and markets.

The company's rating scale ranges from a top grade of AAA for long-term (more than one year) investment-quality instruments to D, for default. AAA, AA, A, and BBB are considered by market participants to be investment-grade ratings. BB, B, CCC, and C are more speculative, and may be considered by market participants to be non–investment-grade ratings. Ratings from AA to CCC may also carry a plus or minus sign to make finer distinctions within a category. The highest rating for short-term issues (less than one year) is A-1. At the bottom of the short-term scale is a D rating.

Besides the letter grade, the outlook for what might happen to the rating over the next six months to two years is represented in four ways—positive (may be raised), negative (may be lowered), stable (unlikely to change), and developing (may be raised or lowered). A numerical rating of 1 to 6 measures the expected recovery of a specific issue that has defaulted. The highest rating is 1+ (the highest expectation of recovery), with 6 indicating negligible recovery after default.

Ratings are based on information supplied by the issuer of the debt or financial obligation and from other reliable sources. A rating is assigned only if adequate information is available. The rating process takes various business, technological, and regulatory factors into account. An issuer's operating and financial plans, along with its management policies, are reviewed, among other things. For sovereign ratings, the country's economic strength, political system, and social environment are examined.

A team of analysts reviews all of the financial data and relevant details before presenting a recommendation to a rating committee composed of senior analysts and others. Each committee member casts one vote. As soon as the committee arrives at a decision, the issuer is notified. If the issuer disagrees with the rating, an appeal can be lodged and may be considered by the agency if additional relevant information is supplied for consideration.

The issuer is monitored on an ongoing basis to see whether any new factors might affect its rating status. These could include important economic developments, changes in capital structure, or new acquisitions. Issuers are expected to notify Standard & Poor's of any significant developments that could have a bearing on its rating. The rating is generally formally reviewed following an annual meeting with the issuer's management.

If a need arises to change a rating, the agency undertakes a preliminary review, and a "CreditWatch" listing may follow. This lets investors know that a new credit rating may be assigned in the near future. After analyzing the new information, the rating committee votes, and the decision is relayed to the issuer, with the same appeals process as above. Ratings may be changed, suspended, or withdrawn at any time the agency deems it necessary.

All of Standard & Poor's ratings are listed on the agency's public website (www.standardandpoors.com).

STANDARD & POOR'S RATING SCALE

AAA	Highest rating, extremely strong capacity to meet financial commitments
AA	Very strong
A	Strong, but can be affected by adverse economic conditions
BBB	Adequate, but more susceptible to adverse economic conditions
BBB	The lowest rating before non–investment grade
BB	Less vulnerable in the near term but more prone to economic conditions
B	More vulnerable to adverse economic conditions but can still meet financial commitments
CCC	Currently vulnerable and dependent on favorable economic conditions to meet financial commitments
CC	Highly vulnerable
C	May be in bankruptcy but payments or financial commitments are continuing
SD	Selective default, failure to pay one or more financial obligations when due
D	Defaulted on financial commitments
NR	Not rated

RATINGS AND BOND PORTFOLIOS

According to a Moody's study of corporate-bond default rates from 1970–2005, the odds of a bond rated Aaa defaulting were tiny—just 0.36 percent within 10 years and 0.64 percent within 20 years. Only about 2 percent of bonds reach this rarified rating.

The further one moves down the scale, the higher the default rate. For A-rated bonds, the expected default rate was 0.87 percent over 10 years and 1.55 percent over 20 years. But at the Caa level, expectations of default rose precipitously—to 14 percent within 10 years and 26 percent within 20 years. That's about 40 times the default rate of Aaa bonds.

Moody's also found that default rates for corporate bonds remained at historic lows during 2007 (0.3 percent), but climbed sharply to 2 percent in 2008 and 5.4 percent in 2009. One of the main reasons for this was the credit crunch associated with the subprime mortgage crisis, which led to a sharp rise in home foreclosures among higher-risk borrowers.

For those who feel that the high interest rates of speculative-grade bonds are too attractive to pass up, the advice is to at least diversify by balancing lower-rated bonds with higher-rated ones. For better protection, they should diversify even more by choosing bonds that are spread across different companies and industries.

Corporate bonds can be downgraded, so if an investment grade bond falls into less desirable territory, it will probably have an undesirable effect on the bond's price. A downgrade occurs when a ratings agency thinks the issuer's credit quality is diminishing. (An investment-grade bond downgraded to non–investment grade is referred to as a *fallen angel.*) Of course, the opposite can also happen, and a rating could be upgraded if the issuer strengthens financially. As a rule, most investors flock to investment-grade bonds during a recession or a depression.

RATING LIMITATIONS

Credit-rating agencies make it crystal clear through disclaimers that ratings are not to be construed as a recommendation to buy or sell a particular security, nor can they predict which issuers might default. Ratings, the agencies maintain, are merely opinions. They address credit risk—the ability of the issuer to fulfill its obligations to make interest payments on time and return the principal at maturity—and not the vagaries of market forces, such as changes in interest rates or a bond's term to maturity, which can affect values.

However, the agencies have been widely criticized for not doing enough to alert investors to the potential pitfalls of subprime mortgage investments. The subprime meltdown then triggered a worldwide financial crisis.

In 2008, the SEC reported that the agencies had "significant weaknesses in their ratings practices for mortgage-backed securities." It said conflicts of interest (that is, a desire for more business and a greater market share) were often behind the high ratings the products received.

Nevertheless, investors rely on ratings as an investment guide to markets or securities about which they may not be very familiar. They help investors navigate their way through the bewildering array of debt-instrument offerings and are useful in determining the degree of an investor's exposure to credit risk.

But investors should bear in mind that ratings are not iron-clad guarantees about an issuer or debt obligation since financial conditions can change over time. Neither are the criteria for rating categories set in stone, meaning there could be slight variations in the credit quality of debt obligations that carry the same rating. Bonds can exhibit wide price movements, even while their ratings remain the same.

Ratings help make the entire financial system more efficient by reducing the costs associated with obtaining reliable credit information, but prudent investors would do well to keep a close check on the status of an issue or an issuer's ratings.

SUMMARY

Credit ratings provide bond investors with a meaningful way of comparing the creditworthiness of one bond over another. Issuers, institutional investors, regulators, and broker-dealers are among the other market participants that rely on credit ratings. Three agencies dominate the field—Moody's, Standard & Poor's, and Fitch Ratings.

Ten credit rating agencies have been designated by the U.S. Securities and Exchange Commission as Nationally Recognized Statistical Rating Organizations (NRSROs), which means their ratings are considered credible for various regulatory purposes.

Before arriving at a rating, credit rating agencies conduct a thorough financial and operational analysis of the issuer or debt instrument. Each agency's ratings are based on a letter grade system, which starts with AAA or Aaa for the top grade and usually ends at D for default.

Ratings on their own are not iron-clad guarantees of creditworthiness since financial conditions may change, and rating agencies themselves have, in some cases, had their ratings judgment questioned, but they remain a major force in the business community.

QUICK QUIZ

1. Explain what investment-grade and non–investment-grade bonds are.
2. Who are the major users of credit ratings?
3. Explain what a Nationally Recognized Statistical Rating Organization is.
4. What does a credit rating measure?
5. What two controversies have dogged the credit-rating industry?
6. What is a *fallen angel*?

4

GOVERNMENT BONDS

Governments are among the world's major issuers of bonds. The U.S. government has the distinction of being the globe's biggest borrower with over US$10 trillion in outstanding U.S. Treasury bonds, (referred to as U.S. Treasuries). Many other nations issue debt instruments known in the marketplace by various names: gilts (United Kingdom), bunds (Germany), Obligations Assimilables du Trésor (OATs) (France) and Japanese Government Bonds (JGBs) (Japan).

U.S. GOVERNMENT DEBT INSTRUMENTS

The main debt instruments issued by the U.S. government through the U.S. Treasury Department are (1) bills, (2) notes, (3) bonds, (4) inflation-protected securities, and (5) savings bonds.

Treasury Bills

Treasury bills (T-bills) are short-term government securities with maturities ranging from a few days to 52 weeks. Bills are sold at a discount from their face value.

They are often classified as *money-market instruments*, since the bills are easily marketable, liquid, and are considered low-risk debt securities.

T-bills are sold at a discount from their stated value and pay no interest before maturity. For example, a US$1,000 T-bill might sell for US$970. The US$1,000 principal returned at maturity would include US$30 earned in interest. A bill can be held until maturity or sold before. Treasury bills are sold at weekly auctions.

Treasury Notes

Treasury notes are government securities that are issued with maturities of 2, 3, 5, 7, and 10 years. Unlike Treasury bills, notes are sold at face value and pay fixed interest rates every six months. For example, if a US$1,000 note has a coupon rate of 5 percent, an investor will get US$25 twice a year. Upon maturity, the principal is returned. The two-year and five-year notes are auctioned monthly; auctions for the 10-year notes are held at various times of the year.

Treasury Bonds

Treasury bonds (T-bonds) are long-term debt obligations, sometimes called *long bonds*, which have a maturity of 30 years and pay interest every six months. Pension funds and institutional investors favor these bonds so as to match the maturity of their investments to obligations to pension members expected to retire many years in the future. From time to time, the government has suspended auctions of such bonds in order to cut borrowing but reintroduced them because of institutional demand.

As with Treasury notes, the face value of a T-bond is returned when the bond matures. Auctions are held four times a year.

Treasury Inflation-Protected Securities (TIPS)

Inflation is a major enemy of fixed-income securities, which is why TIPS were created in 1997. TIPS are securities whose principal is adjusted by changes in the Consumer Price Index. They pay interest every six months and are issued with maturities of 5, 10, and 30 years. The coupon rate remains constant, but the principal is adjusted twice a year to keep pace with the consumer price index (CPI). Thus, the security maintains its value in real-dollar terms. When a TIPS matures, the payment made is the adjusted principal or the original principal, whichever is greater. This again provides protection against deflation. Interest payments will vary because they are based on fluctuating principal amounts. For example, a US$1,000 TIPS with a 4 percent coupon rate would provide an interest payment of US$40 annually, or US$20 semiannually. If, say, the CPI rises by 5 percent, the principal would increase to US$1,050. To calculate the interest on the adjusted amount, the new principal is multiplied by the coupon rate ($1,050 × 4 = $42) and then divided by two ($42/2 = $21) to give the semiannual interest payment. Deflation can cause the principal to be adjusted downward, but it will never fall below the original amount. The effect of the CPI on the principal of a TIPS can be easily calculated at the www.treasurydirect.gov website. However, because of its additional inflation-protection component, the coupon rate on a TIPS is lower than other Treasuries with similar maturities. Another drawback is that, besides having to pay federal income tax on the annual interest, the inflation-adjusted portion of the principal is also taxed annually, even though it's only a paper gain and the security hasn't actually matured or been sold. If inflation is running high, this can have unfavorable tax consequences. Keeping TIPS in tax-protected retirement accounts is one way around the problem. The upside of high inflation is that while other fixed-income investments are losing purchasing power, TIPS retain their value against inflation.

Savings Bonds

Savings bonds are designed for retail investors who are not willing or able to participate in Treasury bond auctions and need a convenient way to purchase government fixed income securities through their bank or payroll savings plans. Interest rates can be found at savings bond websites and are normally changed every May and November based on either current market rates or inflation. There are different types of U.S. savings bonds designated with a letter. For example, an inflation-indexed bond is called an *I Bond* designed to protect purchasing power by offering a real rate of return over and above inflation. They are sold at face value in denominations of \$50, \$75, \$100, \$200, \$500, \$1,000, \$5,000, and \$10,000 and earn interest for as long as 30 years. I Bond dividends earnings are added every month, and interest is compounded semiannually. They are state and local income tax exempt. Most importantly, for U.S. investors, federal income tax on I Bond earnings can be deferred until the bonds are cashed or stop earning interest after 30 years. Investors cashing I Bonds within five years are subject to a 3-month earnings penalty.

The Series EE Savings Bonds pay interest equal to 90 percent of the average of the preceding six-month–5-year Treasury securities yield. Therefore the rates on EE bonds are based on those set by participants in the large government bond trading market. The Series EE bond was a replacement of the E bond, which is most associated with World War II war bonds when the first Series E Bond was purchased by President Franklin D. Roosevelt on May 1, 1941, in a publicity program. During the war, there were many bond sale drives promoted by popular Hollywood celebrities to support the war effort. Those EE bonds were issued in World War I by Liberty Bonds to help that war effort with President Woodrow Wilson taking part in War Bond promotions. A new Series EE "Patriot Bond" was launch in December of 2001 to mark the three-month anniversary of the World Trade Center September 11 terrorist attacks. Money raised from those bond sales was earmarked for the federal government's overall effort to fight the war on global terrorism.

BOND AUCTIONS

Auctions are used by the U.S. Treasury Department to sell their debt instruments (bills, notes, bonds, and TIPS) and fix their rate or yield. Prior to the 1920s the U.S. government offered debt instruments to the market without auctions. This resulted in debt issues being chronically oversubscribed since interest rates offered by the government were so attractive. Purchases of government debt were immediately selling it to other market participants at higher prices. Clearly, the government was paying too much for its debt, and it needed a mechanism to ensure the interest rates they were offering were as low as possible. Therefore in 1929 the U.S. Treasury changed from the fixed-price subscription system to an auction system where the instruments would be sold to the highest bidder so that the market set the prices rather than the government. Now, each year the Treasury conducts over 200 public federal debt auctions. Of course, the value of the Treasuries fluctuates with changes in interest rates and market demand. Investors can participate in an auction and purchase bills, notes, bonds, and TIPS directly from the Treasury, or they can purchase them through a bank or broker who, in turn, participates in the auctions.

The auction process starts when several days before the auction the Treasury announces details of the upcoming issue, including the amount to be auctioned and the maturity date. There are two bidding options, competitive and noncompetitive. In competitive bidding, the buyer specifies the rate he will accept while in noncompetitive bidding the buyer agrees to the rate set at the auction. Once the auction is completed, the Treasury accepts all noncompetitive bids complying with the auction rules and then accepts competitive bids in ascending order from the lowest to the highest yield until all are sold. At the end all bidders, noncompetitive and competitive, receive the same yield at the highest accepted bid.

U.S. TREASURY FUNCTIONS

U.S. Treasuries are the backbone of the international debt industry, not only because of the sheer size of the amount issued but also because the U.S. dollar is the international currency of trade and finance. U.S. Treasuries pay for the operation of the U.S. federal government and finance the public debt; the amount of trading in those instruments also generates large amounts in trading fees for banks and brokers all over the world. Treasury bills, notes, and bonds have been considered virtually risk-free because they are backed by the "full faith and credit" of the United States, which is the world's largest economy and has the strongest military establishment. Because of their perceived safety, U.S. Treasuries normally pay lower interest rates than other bonds around the world. Of course, those conditions could change if there is a change in the perceived strength of the U.S. government and U.S. economy.

The history of U.S. government debt goes back to the Continental Congress, the meeting of the British colonies who declared independence from England and began issuing debt securities in 1776. Ever since that time, the United States has had outstanding debts. The person considered to have done much to establish the United States as a safe investment was the visionary first secretary of the treasury, Alexander Hamilton, who established sound goals and principles for debt management. Over the years, U.S. Treasuries developed important characteristics of being default risk-free, with a seamless yield curve, lots of liquidity, and low bid-ask spreads. These characteristics enabled Treasuries to perform economic functions separate from only financing past federal budget deficits.

Probably the most important of Treasuries' economic functions is how the Federal Reserve uses Treasuries to conduct U.S. monetary policy. Also, foreign central banks hold Treasuries as a store of value and a means to intervene in their foreign-exchange markets. Over the years, Treasuries have become the premier safe haven investment during economic turbulence. Traders and investors use the Treasury bond yield curve as the pricing benchmark for other bonds. Even the U.S. government indexes its loans to students and farmers to Treasury yields. Treasuries collateralize a large part of the transactions in the repurchase agreement (repo) market. In the pension arena, the government's Pension Benefit Guaranty Corporation (PBGC) utilizes the 30-year Treasury bond yield to determine if the funding of private pension plans is adequate.

The major credit-rating agencies give U.S. Treasuries their highest rating. U.S. Treasuries are held by international banks, pension funds, multinational corporations, foreign governments, and insurance companies.

U.S. Treasury securities are highly liquid debt instruments and are actively traded in the secondary market so that investors are free to sell their Treasuries at any time before they mature. (*Note*: U.S. savings bonds are a different debt type and cannot be sold to other buyers.) Yields on Treasury notes and bonds are considered bellwether indicators, and their price levels are watched closely by bond market traders and investors as a predictor of where the cost of what is considered risk-free capital is heading. Only governments can issue default-free securities because of their ability to tax and control the money supply. This, of course, does not mean that governments will not default on their debt, even if denominated in their own currency. The Russian government defaulted on their ruble bonds in 1998, for example.

STRIPS

Separate Trading of Registered Interest and Principal Securities, or STRIPS, were created by the financial industry to have another marketable and traded security. They are T-Notes, T-Bonds, and TIPS whose interest and principal portions of the security have been separated, or *stripped*. These separate portions may be sold, in the secondary market normally in units of $1,000 face value. The name originates from the time before computerization when paper bonds were physically traded and traders would actually clip the interest coupons off the paper bonds to sell separately. The result is the creation of a type of zero-coupon or *deep discount* bond that pays no periodic interest. STRIPS are popular with investors because these securities allow them to obtain the earnings of Treasury bills and bonds without a large initial outlay of capital. Since STRIPS are zero-coupon securities the investor knows in advance what the future value of the investment will be, since the STRIP will always pay its face value at maturity and the investor's return will be the difference between the face value and the discounted price he paid for it. The return is predictable and can be used for financial planning. A standard bond can be less predictable since if such a bond is called by the issuer and paid in advance the investor would lose the amount of interest the bond would have paid until maturity.

STRIPS also have the advantage over normal Treasury securities in that they offer a variety of maturity dates since they can be based on interest payments. Thus, the investor does not need to wait a long time for maturity, and he can choose from a variety of maturity dates offering different returns. An additional advantage is that STRIPS returns are automatic interest reinvestment so there is no reinvestment risk or a risk that the cash flow produced by the investment would need to be reinvested at a lower rate of return.

U.S. GOVERNMENT AGENCY BONDS

In addition to debt instruments issued by the U.S. Treasury, there are bonds issued by government-related organizations, departments, or agencies. Such bonds include those issued by (1) official federal agencies and (2) government-sponsored enterprises (GSEs). Since these agency bonds do not carry the full guarantee or faith and credit of the U.S. government, they tend to offer higher yields than Treasuries. Many investors believe that if there is a default by a federal agency the government will assume a moral obligation to pay the loans in full. During the subprime crisis of 2008, the U.S. government seized control of two insolvent government-sponsored organizations, the Federal National Mortgage Association (Fannie Mae) and the Federal Home Loan Mortgage Corporation (Freddie Mac), thus guaranteeing the debts of the two mortgage giants, even though legally the government could have walked away. Other government-affiliated organizations that have issued debt instruments in addition to Fannie Mae and Freddie Mac include the Federal Home Loan Bank System (FHLB or "Home Loan"), Federal Farm Credit Bank (FFCB or "Farm Credit"), the Government National Mortgage Association (GNMA or "Ginnie Mae"), the Student Loan Marketing Association (SLMA or "Sallie Mae"), and the Tennessee Valley Authority (TVA).

Most agency bonds pay interest semiannually. Some are callable, which allows the agency to buy back the bond before it matures. Interest rates on such callable bonds are normally higher. Agency bond maturities can range up to 30 years. Agency bonds can be structured to meet several different specific needs; in addition to the traditional coupon-paying agency bond, some organizations issue no-coupon discount rate bonds, step-up notes, and floaters:

Discos: Some agencies offer no-coupon discount rate bonds (or *discos*). These shorter-term bonds (with maturities from one day to one year) are similar to zero-coupon bonds because they sell at a discount and pay interest and principal at maturity.

Step-Up Notes: Another type of agency bond is a *step-up* note where the coupon rate is adjusted upward at certain intervals, allowing investors the satisfaction of gaining more interest as time goes on. These can also be callable.

Floaters: A *floater* bond is one in which the interest or coupon rate varies from month to month based on a short-term benchmark, such as U.S. Treasury bill rates.

U.S. MUNICIPAL BONDS

In addition to federal government–related fixed-income instruments, there is a big variety of municipal bond instruments (called munis) issued by cities, states, airports, and municipalities, who issue bonds to raise money for ongoing expenditures or for capital investments such as roads, water and sewerage systems, bridges, airports, and others. Since they are related to a local government entity, and not the federal government, they normally offer a high degree of safety but not as high as the federal government. Their interest rates would thus tend to be higher than federally issued instruments. (A study of bond defaults by credit-rating agency Moody's over the 30-year period between 1970 and 2000 listed 18 municipal-bond defaults (all of them revenue bonds) compared with 819 corporate-bond defaults.)

There are generally three types of munis: (1) general obligation bonds, (2) revenue bonds, and (3) pre-refunded/escrowed-to-maturity bonds.

General obligation bonds: These bonds are secured by the local government or entity's taxing ability rather than from earnings from a particular project. Thus voters in the municipality, town, or state must normally approve these bonds before they are issued. Since such bonds are a direct obligation of the local government authority, they are preferable to many investors, and this preference has been rewarded since defaults of general obligation bonds have been quite infrequent.

Revenue bonds: The returns of interest and principal of these bonds depend on the revenues, tolls, charges, or mortgage rents from public works projects, such as highways, bridges, stadiums, or other facilities. Since they are not dependent on tax income, they do not require voter approval. Revenue bonds have been issued for hospitals, higher educational institutions, housing, airports, electric power projects, and other such facilities. Since repayment of interest and principal from such bonds depends on project revenues, unreliable revenues could have a negative impact on the issuer's ability to meet the bond payments.

Pre-refunded/escrowed-to-maturity bonds: These are rather complicated instruments, which at some point transform from being supported by the original issuer to being supported by the U.S. government. This can happen in an environment of falling interest rates, when a municipality wants to take advantage of cheaper rates—similar to a homeowner who refinances a mortgage.

One of the key appeals of municipal bonds in the United States is that they are exempt from federal taxes. In addition, if they are bought by a resident of the state that issued the bond, they can also be exempt from state and local taxes. This tax advantage feature enables state and local governments to sometimes borrow at lower rates than corporations and sometimes even the federal government.

Although the big attraction of munis is the tax-exempt feature, there are taxable municipal bonds in existence. These bonds attract federal taxes when the federal government decides that the project for which funds need to be raised does not significantly benefit the public at large. However they are still exempt from state or local taxes. The interest rates on such bonds are more in line with those of other taxable bonds.

MUNICIPAL BONDS WITH SPECIAL FEATURES

There are four types of municipal bonds with special features, including:

1. *Insured bonds:* Some municipal bonds have an insurance feature where an insurance company takes responsibility for the payment of interest and principal in case of a default. This perceived safety factor is often reflected in a slightly lower yield than offered by uninsured municipal bonds.

2. *Floating-rate/variable-rate bonds:* Interest rates for these bonds are periodically adjusted and based upon the going rate for U.S. Treasuries or other securities.

3. *Put bonds:* Investors in these bonds have the right to *put* or redeem these bonds at par value before the maturity date, enabling the bondholder to reinvest the principal in higher-yielding bonds.

4. *Capital-appreciation bonds (CABS):* These bonds are zero-coupon and sold at a steep discount from their face value so that the bond matures at face value with the interest earned being tax-free.

Most municipal bonds are rated by major rating agencies, such as Moody's, Standard & Poor's, and Fitch. Munis that are not rated can be riskier and more illiquid than those that are. As a rule, the lower the rating, the more volatile the bond.

Some municipal bonds are callable, which means that the issuer can demand redemption at some point before the bond matures. This usually happens at the best time for the issuer and the least-opportune time for bondholders; that is, when interest rates are falling and the price of the bond is rising. Callable bonds pay slightly more, but the uncertainty involved for investors may not be worth it.

BUYING MUNICIPAL BONDS

Municipal bonds must be purchased through a broker (intermediary). To see if the price a broker is offering is fair, a number of websites (www.municipalbonds.com, www.investinginbonds.com, and www.finra.org, for example) provide information about past transaction prices for individual bonds. Ask the broker for the bond's CUSIP (Committee on Uniform Security Identification Procedures) number to make searching for the bond easier.

MORTGAGE-BACKED SECURITIES

Mortgage-backed securities (MBSs) are mortgages that are grouped into US$25–$50 million pools and parceled off to investors. They have become increasingly popular in recent years. In the United States, the monthly mortgage payments that homeowners make are passed through to bondholders as a monthly income. MBSs are an important source of funds for Ginnie Mae, Freddie Mac, and Fannie Mae. Asset-backed securities operate in a similar manner, except that instead of mortgages, the assets can be credit card, auto, boat, or other types of loans.

MBSs can be complicated and lack the income consistency of other bonds. Agency MBSs must meet Federal National Mortgage Association underwriting requirements, whereas the creditworthiness of private-sector MBSs is left to the judgment of each issuing company. (See Chapter 5 for a more in-depth discussion of MBSs and their role in the subprime mortgage crisis.)

FOREIGN GOVERNMENT BONDS

Investing in bonds issued by foreign governments provides diversification and a potential opportunity for higher returns. However there are two major risks: currency and sovereign default.

1. *Currency risk:* This refers to fluctuations in exchange rates that could affect an investment's value if the country's bonds are issued in local currency. This is why a great deal of sovereign debt is issued in U.S. dollars to eliminate the currency risk and make the bonds more attractive to investors.

2. *Sovereign risk:* This is the risk that a foreign government will default or will issue regulations or take actions that could decrease a bond's value. For example, governmental actions such as quotas and tariffs could detrimentally affect a country's export and import trade, reduce government income, and result in an inability to repay debt. Or a war or revolution could render the government incapable of handling its own finances or even lead to it refusing to honor its obligations.

Bonds from developed nations tend to have interest rates that are highly correlated with those from the United States (meaning they tend to move in the same direction). Those from emerging markets may be less correlated while, at the same time, possibly offering the prospect of greater price appreciation and interest income. However, investors should be prepared to bear greater risks for such higher returns.

United Kingdom

UK gilts are marketable bonds issued in pounds sterling by the United Kingdom government. Similar to U.S. Treasuries, they normally pay interest semiannually, with repayment of the principal in full at maturity.

There are three categories of gilts: (1) short-dated (0–7 years), (2) medium-dated (7–15 years), and (3) long-dated (15 years or more). *Ultra-short* gilts have maturities of three years or less, while gilts with 40 years or more left to maturity are considered *ultra-long*.

New gilts are issued by the UK Debt Management Office (DMO), an executive agency of Her Majesty's Treasury, under the same type of competitive and noncompetitive auction bidding process as in the United States. Computershare Investor Services maintains the register of holdings of gilts under a contract from Her Majesty's Treasury and is administered by the DMO.

The largest portion of gilts consists of conventional debt instruments where the investors receive regular interest payments and the return of their principal at a fixed maturity date. The other major type of gilt issued is the index-linked gilt. These offer market interest rates, but the semiannual coupon and principal repayment are linked to movements in the UK's Retail Price Index.

Other types of gilts representing a small portion of the total include:

- *Double-dated:* bonds that are issued with two redemption dates and can be redeemed at the government's discretion at any time between the two dates, subject to three months' notice.

- *Undated:* the redemption of which is also at the option of the government. However, because of their age (some date back to the eighteenth century), they all have low coupons, and so there is little incentive for the government to redeem them.

- *Gilt STRIPS*, which were introduced in 1997, are similar to U.S. Treasury STRIPS, in that their coupon payments and principal can be stripped apart and traded separately.

France

France's government debt is managed by Agence France Trésor (AFT), which handles public debt and treasury management for the French government. In 2001 it was created by a Ministry of the Economy, Finance and Industry (currently the Ministry of the Economy, Industry and Employment) as a department reporting to the head of the Treasury Directorate (today head of the Treasury and Economic Policy Directorate).

France has three categories of standardized debt securities denominated in euros, which are distinguishable by their maturities and offered via a bid-price auction system:

- *Bons du Trésor à taux fixe et à intérêts précomtés* (BTFs) are fixed-rate discount Treasury bills with a maturity of less than one year.

- *Bons du Trésor à interêts annuels* (BTANs) are fixed-rate, medium-term Treasury notes, with maturities of either two or five years.

- *Obligations Assimilables du Trésor* (OATs) are long-term debt securities with maturities from 7 to 50 years. Most OATs have fixed-rate coupons, but some are floating-rate or inflation-indexed instruments.

Germany

The German government issues a wide range of debt securities, denominated in euros. Standard issues include federal bonds (*Bunds*), five-year federal notes (*Bobls*), federal treasury notes (*Schätze*), federal savings notes (*Bundesschatzebriefe*), federal treasury financing paper (*Finanzierungsschätze*), and treasury discount paper. Foreign-currency bonds, inflation-linked Germany government securities, and German-type promissory notes have been added in recent years.

Most feature a fixed coupon with annual interest payments. Anyone may purchase federal bonds, federal notes, and federal Treasury notes, which are listed on German stock exchanges. Federal savings notes are unlisted and restricted to natural persons and resident institutions serving public, charitable, or religious purposes.

- Federal bonds (*Bundesanleihen* or *Bunds*) are long-term bonds issued at maturities of 10 and 30 years and play an important role in the German capital market. Generally, no minimum or maximum investment amount applies.

- Five-year federal notes (*Bundesobligationen* or *Bobls*) are medium-term instruments with a maturity of five years.

- Federal treasury notes (*Bundesschatzanweisungen* or *Schätze*) have a maturity of two years.

Federal savings notes, introduced in 1969 to promote individual savings in Germany, come in two varieties: Type A matures in six years and pays interest annually; Type B, with a seven-year maturity, accumulates annual and compound interest, and is paid as a single sum upon maturity. Minimum investment is €50.

Japan

Japanese government securities include government bonds, which are issued in yen with maturities of 2 to 40 years, and pay interest semiannually. While government bonds are listed on all Japanese stock exchanges, virtually all trading is done over the counter. Issuance is by competitive and non-bidding at public auctions.

Japanese bonds are classified into six categories:

1. Short-term (six-month and one-year Treasury bills)—discount bonds, which pay no interest but return their full face value at maturity.

2. Medium-term—two-year and five-year fixed-rate bonds.

3. Long-term—10-year fixed-rate bonds.

4. Super-long-term—15-year floating-rate bonds, and 20-year and 40-year fixed-rate bonds.

5. Government bonds for individual investors—5-year fixed-rate and 10-year floating-rate bonds sold at minimum face values of ¥10,000.

6. Inflation-indexed bonds—10-year bonds that pay a fixed coupon rate but whose principal amount is linked to the Consumer Price Index (CPI). Thus, the interest payment fluctuates.

SUMMARY

Government debt is the rock upon which the global fixed-income market is based. The United States leads the world in the sheer volume of its borrowing. U.S. Treasuries are virtually risk-free because the U.S. government has never defaulted on its loans. The four main U.S. Treasuries are Treasury bills, Treasury notes, Treasury bonds, and Treasury Inflation Protected Securities (TIPS).

For new investors, U.S. savings bonds offer a good introduction to fixed-income securities and can be purchased for as little as US$25. STRIPS are a type of zero-coupon bond that consist of various kinds of U.S. Treasuries whose coupons and final principal payment are stripped from the security and sold separately.

Other countries offer their own versions of government debt, such as UK gilts, German Bunds, French OATs, and Japanese JGBs. Many have also followed the United States in issuing their own STRIPS.

Municipal bonds issued by cities, states, municipal utilities, and so on raise money for current expenditures or for capital projects while offering appealing tax-exempt features. Agency bonds from official federal agencies and government-sponsored enterprises provide loans to homeowners, farmers, small businesses, and others.

QUICK QUIZ

1. Describe the four types of U.S. Treasuries.
2. Explain why only governments can issue risk-free securities.
3. How do UK gilts differ from U.S. Treasuries?
4. For what purpose were TIPS created?
5. What are the main functions of municipal bonds and agency bonds?

5
CORPORATE BONDS

A corporate bond is simply a bond issued by a corporation to raise debt finance. Corporate bonds are normally longer-term debt instruments with maturity dates at least one year after the initial issue. ("Commercial paper" is the term used for shorter-dated corporate debt issues.)

The line between corporate and government bonds often becomes blurred since there are a number of instances where a government-owned corporation issues a bond. Strictly speaking such a bond is a corporate bond, but since it is issued by a government-owned company, it might be considered to have the added safety of a government bond.

The corporate bond market is big business. Each day, an estimated US$17 billion in corporate bonds are traded in the United States alone, and over US$7 trillion of corporate bond obligations are outstanding. Over 5,000 companies issue corporate bonds. These bonds are mainly traded over the counter through bond dealers and brokers who trade by phone or electronically.

The corporate bond market is dominated by institutional investors, but individuals also participate. Major issuers of corporate bonds include public utilities, transportation companies, industrial corporations, financial-services companies, and conglomerates.

USES OF CORPORATE BONDS

For companies, corporate bonds offer a means of raising funds without having to sell shares in their company and thus diluting existing shareholdings. Issuing bonds can also be cheaper than going to a bank and obtaining a loan. Companies use the proceeds from their bonds for various purposes, such as building factories, buying equipment, or even buying back their own common stock to enhance the price of their stock on the exchange.

Looking at it from the lender's (or creditor's) point of view, investors are attracted to bonds because they know that in the event of a company failure they will be paid ahead of the company's shareholders. Bondholders rank higher than holders of common stock when it comes to liquidating the company's assets.

Corporate bonds thus provide a measure of safety that shares of stock often do not. Of course, bond investors do not participate in company growth and profitability since, in return for loaning money, they receive fixed-interest payments and repayment of their principal at maturity.

CORPORATE BOND RISKS

Although corporate bonds do provide a measure of safety, any investment comes with risks; corporate bond risks include default risks, credit risk spread, interest rate risk, liquidity risk, supply/demand risk, and inflation risk.

Default Risk

History shows that defaults of corporate bonds tend to occur more frequently than for sovereign or government bonds. Of course, this is a gross generalization since a corporate bond issued by a strong company could have a substantially lower risk of default compared to some heavily indebted countries. Nevertheless, since corporate bonds tend to have a higher yield, the perceived high risk is compensated.

Credit Spread Risk

This is when the spread or difference between the yield of the corporate bond falls too low, so as not to compensate for the risk of default. This occurs when the market price of the bond rises so that the yield falls and is lower than a higher-rated bond. This, of course, can be adjusted if the bond price falls so that the yield rises to a level that will compensate for the default risk.

Interest Rate Risk

If the general interest rates of bonds, in particular government bonds, changes, this has an impact on corporate bonds, thus creating a risk. A rise in government bond rates would be negative for fixed-rate corporate bonds, since their price would tend to fall, resulting in a higher yield in line with the rising government bond yields.

Liquidity Risk

Corporate bonds can be listed or unlisted. Many corporate bonds are often listed on major exchanges. However most of the trading volume of corporate bonds is executed over the counter in decentralized, dealer-based operations. Since a significant portion of corporate bonds are traded over the counter, there may not be a very liquid market for the bonds, so that investors attempting to exit the bonds would be at the mercy of the broker market makers and forced to accept an unfairly low price.

Supply/Demand Risk

Big increases in bond issues could result in a general fall in prices for all bonds and impact corporate bond holders.

Inflation Risk

A rise in inflation increases the risk for bond holders with fixed-rate bonds, since their interest earnings may not keep up with generally rising prices. Any hint of impending inflation increases can send bond prices downward.

TYPES OF CORPORATE BONDS

Corporate bonds are categorized as secured or unsecured.

Secured bonds are backed by some form of collateral, such as real estate, financial assets, or transportation equipment. For example, when one corporation guarantees the bonds of another corporation, these are called (not surprisingly) *guaranteed bonds.* A parent company might guarantee the bonds of a subsidiary, for example, and thus reap the benefits of its more established name and credit standing.

Unsecured bonds have no such collateral guarantee and are only backed by an issuer's good name or credit standing. The key is the issuer's ability to repay interest and principal, rather than by pledging of assets.

Under these two general categories, there is a wide variety of corporate bonds explained below. Of course, the creativity of bankers, brokers, and companies knows no bounds, so we should not be surprised that the descriptions below are not comprehensive, since new types of bonds continue to be created.

Covered Bonds

These are a type of secured bond backed by cash flows from such instruments as mortgages, government securities, or loans. They resemble asset-backed securities that are created when groups of bonds are combined in a security, but in the case of covered bonds, the assets remain on the issuer's consolidated balance sheet, while in the case of asset-backed securities they are sold on to investors and do not remain on the balance sheet of the issuer. So, in essence a covered bond is a type of corporate bond with one significant difference: In the event that the issues become insolvent, the covered bond holder has legal recourse to the pool of assets that secures or *covers* the bond issued. As a result of that feature, covered bonds are often assigned high credit ratings. The significant advantage to the investor is that the debt and underlying pool of assets remains in the issuer's accounts, and the issuer must ensure that the asset pools continuously will support the covered bond. If there is a default, the investor can claim the asset pool and also has further recourse to the issuer. Another advantage is that interest payments come from a clearly defined cash flow source so that if loans covering the bond become nonperforming, for example, they must be replaced in the pool with performing loans.

NOTE
PFANDBRIEF

The first idea of a covered bond was the Pfandbrief (plural Pfandbriefe) introduced in 1769 in Prussia during the reign of Frederick the Great. After the disastrous Seven Years' War, which lasted from 1756 to 1763 and devastated Prussia, Frederick the Great introduced the Pfandbrief system in order to ease the shortage of credit available to the nobility. The Prussian government established public law associations of noble landowners, called Landschaften, for the purpose of refinancing loans to their members. The Landschaften issued securities where the buyers of those securities had a claim over the estates the lender member had pledged as security. This Pfandbrief system spread throughout all of Europe, and at the end of the nineteenth century it was widely adopted for public sector loan refinancing, becoming the model for covered bonds. Today this type of security has been introduced in most European countries and is a model for covered bonds in other parts of the world.

Asset-Backed Bonds

Asset-backed bonds represent are a growing segment of the fixed-income market that are collateralized by various kinds of assets and can be any type of receivable, such as home-equity loans, credit-card debt, auto loans, boat loans, or equipment leases. The rock star David Bowie created a stir in 1997 by issuing his own 10-year bond, using future royalties from his first 25 albums recorded before 1990 as collateral. Investors went along to the tune of US$55 million. The bond's yield was 7.9 percent, but the fickleness of record buyers added to the level of risk.

Convertible Bonds

Convertible bonds allow investors to convert the bond into equity. They are a hybrid between a bond and equity since they begin life as a conventional corporate bond, but at some future point the bond can be converted into shares of common stock. Thus, a bondholder (lender) can become a stockholder (part-owner of the company) and benefit from the future growth and profits of the company.

Like a traditional bond, convertibles pay interest annually or, more frequently, have a fixed maturity date, and may be callable, which means that the issuing company can buy back the bonds. The extra feature of convertible bonds is that if the company's stock price rises, the bondholder may choose to benefit from capital appreciation (provided that the company does not *call* the bond) by converting the bond into shares. Bondholders are under no obligation to do so and may simply continue to receive steady interest income.

Corporations issue convertible bonds because they can usually be issued at a much lower interest rate than normal bonds since the conversion feature adds a kicker benefit to the holders. These bonds also allow firms to raise capital without having to immediately add a huge number of new shares to their pool of common stock. Additionally, the lower interest rate makes convertible bonds less costly for companies to service. If the company issues shares rather than convertible bonds, the sudden addition of more new shares results in a dilution of a company's equity, which can be unsettling to investors who see their piece of the pie shrinking. When a convertible bond is issued, a conversion ratio used to calculate the number of shares of stock that the bond can be exchanged for is stated in the bond prospectus. The conversion ratio is found by dividing the bond's par value by the conversion price or *strike price*. Most often, this is much higher than the price of the stock at the time the convertible bond was offered since the issuing company does not want to allow the buyers to get the shares too cheap and lower or equal to the prevailing market price.

If we assume that the par value of the bond is $1,000 and the conversion price is $100 per share, this works out to 10 shares of common stock per $1,000 bond, or a ratio of 10:1.

Par value/Conversion price = $1,000/$100 = 10 shares

Assume that the price of the stock was $70 when the convertible bond was issued, but that it has since risen to $115 per share. Since the conversion or strike price is $100, the convertible bond holders are now at an advantage. When they purchased the bond, the market price of the stock was $70, but the conversion price was $100, so converting at any price up to $100 would not yield a profit and the conversion price was out-of-the-money, but now that the share price has risen to $115, conversion is advantageous to the bond holder and will yield a profit. Conversion parity occurs when the stock price equals the conversion price—in this case, $100. But at $115 per share, a $15 capital gain per share can be realized. By holding onto the shares, the investor is in a good position if the price continues to increase, but stands to lose if the price falls below $100. If the convertible bond is callable (this could occur if the price of the stock rose to some predetermined level for a certain period of time), the corporation normally would be required to give bondholders the chance to convert to shares before calling in the bonds.

Convertibles are popular among investors because they have limited downside risk (the bond still pays interest and repays the principal at maturity even if the stock price goes through the floor) and unlimited upside potential (no ceiling theoretically exists on the company's stock price). Convertible bond prices depend not only on the interest rate yield of the bond but also on the difference between the strike price of the bond shares and the market price of the shares. An increase in the underlying stock price will increase the value of the call on the stock and increase the value of the convertible bond.

Original Issue Discount Bonds

Some corporate bonds may be issued a lower price than their face (par) value. That difference is called the *original-issue discount.* Zero-coupon bonds are the most common type of this bond.

Trust Bonds

There are different types of trust bonds. Collateralized trust bonds are bonds backed by assets such as stocks or bonds of companies other than the issuing company. Equipment trust certificates are bonds issued by companies such as airlines and railroads to pay for new equipment. A trustee retains the title to the equipment until full payment is made, after which the corporation assumes ownership.

Junk Bonds

The term *junk bond* refers to high-yielding bonds rated below investment grade (lower than Ba or BB by rating agencies such as Moody's or Standard & Poor's), which puts it at higher risk of default. Many consider these bonds strictly for speculators. Nevertheless, historical returns for junk bonds have averaged 4–6 percent above those for comparable U.S Treasuries.

Junk bonds or to use the less-pejorative term, *high-yield bonds*, are issued by companies that are either fairly new and haven't established much of a credit history or that possess somewhat of a dubious credit past. They might be issued by vibrant start-ups, businesses that have seen better days, or better-known companies that are heavily in debt. The bonds pay high interest rates because otherwise no one would take the risk of buying them. However, high-yield bonds are off-limits to many pension funds, banks, and insurance companies because these institutions are prohibited from investing in anything other than investment-grade debt. Investment-grade issues can have terms up to 30 years, while junk-bond maturities are much shorter (usually 5 to 10 years).

Various types of junk bonds have been given colorful names by bond traders. A *fallen angel* is a bond that once had investment-grade status but has been downgraded because of concerns about the issuing firm's ability to service its debts. A *rising star* is a bond whose credit rating is moving toward investment quality because of the improving credit quality of the issuing company.

Many high-yield bonds are issued as private placements directly to institutional investors rather than as public offerings, thus bypassing individual

NEWS CLIP
THE EMERGENCE OF JUNK BONDS

Junk bonds rose to prominence in the 1980s when Michael Milken, of the now-bankrupt investment banking house Drexel Burnham Lambert, and other junk-bond kings, created empires based on these less-than-stellar debt securities. During that era, the bonds were a favorite financing technique for a raft of hostile takeovers and acquisitions. The market began to collapse in 1989 after several proposed high-profile deals fell through amidst a rising tide of defaults by junk-bond issuers. Earning between US$200 million and US$550 million a year at the height of his success, Milken amassed a great personal fortune. However, in 1989 he was indicted for securities fraud by a federal grand jury and spent almost two years in prison after pleading guilty to securities and reporting violations. He was banned for life from the securities industry.

NOTE
INVESTMENT GRADE AS AN ECONOMIC INDICATOR

In Chapter 3, we discussed rating agencies and noted that *investment grade* refers to safer, high-quality bonds, which are rated Baa or BBB or higher. Companies that issue investment-grade bonds are considered financially healthy, with the result that investors have little fear they will default. Investment-grade corporate bonds are not risk-free, however. The element of risk is the reason why they pay more than comparable U.S. Treasuries. This is known as the *investment-grade spread* or *risk premium*. Within the trade, the spread is closely observed as an economic indicator: The wider the spread, the worse the state of the economy. Overall, corporate bonds have historically paid about more than Treasuries of similar maturity to compensate for the additional risk. The investment-grade bond market is much larger than the high-yield bond market, even though the latter has had far more publicity.

investors. This occurs much less frequently with investment-grade bonds. Despite their history, high-yield bonds remain a viable part of the corporate bond market. They provide a source of capital for companies and diversification for investors.

Callable Bonds

These corporate bonds include a call option, allowing the issuer to redeem the debt before the maturity date. Like Treasuries, municipal, and government agency bonds, corporate bonds may be callable; that is, the issuer can repurchase the bond at a specified call price. Obviously, it is in the best interests of the firm to call a bond if interest rates are falling, since this gives the company an opportunity to save what could add up to millions of dollars in interest by re-issuing new bonds at a lower coupon rate.

When a bond is called, bondholders are in the sometimes frustrating position of having to reinvest their proceeds at a lower rate somewhere else. One saving grace is that callable bonds tend to pay a bit more interest (the *call premium*) than noncallable bonds.

Bondholders are normally given 30 days' notice of a bond call. In many cases, the amount they receive is par value, or what the principal repayment would be at maturity, although some pay slightly higher premiums. The sacrifice is the loss of the bond's remaining coupon payments at the higher interest rate.

Callability is written into the bond contract, so there is no way to eliminate the risk. But certain conditions must be observed. For example, a bond contract might say that a 20-year bond may only be called 10 years after it has been issued. On the other hand, a callable bond might never be called, particularly if interest rates rise.

An early call will obviously affect the bond's yield to maturity, so it's necessary to know what the yield to call is. The price of a callable bond should be equal to a similar straight or noncallable bond, minus the price of the call option. Therefore the price of a callable bond is always lower and the yield higher than a straight bond, because the call option gives added value to the issuer.

Put Bonds

Put bonds give the investor the option of *putting* the bond back to the issuer and cashing it in, either once during the term of the bond or on a number of specific dates before maturity. One-time puts are more common than puts that feature a series of redemption dates. The bonds can be sold back to the issuer at a price that is fixed at the time of issue, usually at par. This is useful if the bond is trading at less than par value when the option is exercised. An investor might also decide to redeem a put bond to take advantage of prevailing higher interest rates so he can take the money received and place it in a bond with a higher interest rate.

However, the coupon rate on puts is lower than for callable bonds because the issuing company faces some uncertainty about whether an investor will hang on to the bond or redeem it early. Much less common than callable bonds, put bonds are also known as *multimaturity bonds*, *option-tender bonds*, and *variable-rate demand obligations*. The price of a puttable bond should be equal to a straight bond plus the price of the put option. Therefore the price of a puttable bond is always higher than the price of a straight bond because the put option adds value to the bondholder. Therefore, the yield on a puttable bond should be lower than the yield of a straight bond. An increase in interest rate volatility will increase the value of the put option and increase the value of the puttable bond.

Sinking Fund Bonds

Sinking fund bonds or *sinkable* bonds contain sinking fund provisions where the issuer puts interest and principal payments aside into a dedicated sinking fund account and periodically pays out or retires portions of the bond issue's outstanding debt. Sometimes the timing of individual payments is determined by a lottery, leaving investors at the mercy of chance as to whether their bonds will be redeemed at a certain time or not. Such unpredictable payout timings or compulsory bond redemptions means that the investor may lose out on the opportunity to make a profit if the secondary-market price exceeds the redemption price (usually par). Another alternative is a pro rata *sinker*, in which an equal percentage of bonds are redeemed from each bondholder at specific times.

Bullet Bonds

Bullet bonds are neither callable nor puttable and make regular interest payments, and repay their principal at maturity. The interest rate on a bullet bond is lower than for a callable bond, since the investor is protected against early redemption calls if interest rates decline.

Socially Responsible Bonds

Investors can salve their consciences and earn money at the same time by investing in bonds from ethical companies that promote environmentalism, consumer protection, and quality products. Such bonds typically steer clear of companies associated with sin industries (tobacco, alcohol, gambling), weapons production, or companies accused of human-rights violations. There is growing interest in such socially responsible investing, and some studies indicate that bond funds in this sector performed as well or better than conventional bonds.

Church Bonds Church bonds date back more than a century and have been issued to build or upgrade church property, which serves as the collateral for the bonds. Many are private offerings, but some are open to the general public. According to some studies, church bonds have proved their mettle as financially rewarding investments, with yields slightly more than investment-grade corporate bonds.

However, since church bonds are not actively traded, those who don't hold them for their full term might be disappointed if they can't sell them. The bonds are also normally callable, so their full benefit may not be realized if the bonds are called in early.

Sukuk Issued mainly in Islamic countries, *sukuk* are *Shari'ah*-compliant bonds. The Islamic faith prohibits paying or charging interest. Therefore, holders of *sukuk* are considered beneficial owners in the underlying assets. Like traditional bonds, *sukuk* make regular payments on the amount of principal invested but these payments are considered to come from a share in the revenues generated by the *sukuk*'s assets (property, equipment, and so on) rather than from the concept of interest. The market for *sukuk* is growing, with Malaysia, the United Arab Emirates, and Bahrain among the leading players.

Catastrophe Bonds Catastrophe bonds, or CATS, are issued by insurers who want to raise funds in the event of a disaster like a hurricane, an earthquake, or a flood. If a disaster strikes and the insurer becomes inundated with claims, interest payments and/or repayment of the principal can be deferred or stopped. Catastrophe bonds pay attractive rates of return and also provide diversification, and an investment that is unaffected by stock or corporate bond movements. But investors are essentially taking a gamble on the forces of nature.

MORTGAGE BONDS AND MORTGAGE-BACKED SECURITIES

Mortgage bonds are corporate bonds secured by liens on real estate or other physical property, while mortgage-backed securities (MBS) are bonds backed by a pool of mortgages. In the United States, the large housing agencies such as Ginnie Mae and Freddie Mac have been the major MBS issuers, but there are other issuers as well. The MBS mortgage pools are sold to investors who receive monthly income (as opposed to the semiannual payments from conventional bonds) on the mortgage payments made by homeowners. Mortgage-backed securities are also called *pass-through* because the interest and principal from the homeowner is passed through to the bondholder. In recent years, private MBSs began accepting riskier subprime mortgages, even though they posed a higher credit risk. Investors flocked to these debt instruments until 2007, when falling home prices and foreclosures led to defaults and declining market values of the securities. This led to the 2007–2008 credit crisis that reverberated around the world.

Formulating MBSs and CDOs

After homeowners obtain their mortgages, the lending bank of the financial institution sells its loan portfolio to a mortgage broker, who packages the

NEWS CLIP
THE SUBPRIME MORTGAGE CRISIS

Housing foreclosures from subprime mortgages in late 2006 triggered a serious global financial crisis in 2007 and 2008. Earlier, subprime mortgages with adjustable teaser interest rates had been granted to borrowers with weak credit, often with no down payment or proof of income. By March 2007, the value of U.S. subprime mortgages was estimated at US$1.3 trillion. Spurred on by steadily rising housing prices and a buoyant economy, banks and other financial institutions kept aggressively lending money to home buyers. Borrowers took on mortgages that they couldn't afford, often obtaining interest-only loans in order to keep their monthly payments low. If they decided to refinance their mortgages later, many erroneously thought they could count on the appreciating value of their homes to negotiate better terms. But starting in 2006 housing prices in the United States began to falter just as adjustable-rate mortgage interest rates began to reset much higher, pushing many borrowers into negative equity (homes were worth less than what was paid for them) as payments rose beyond their means. In 2007, foreclosure proceedings were instituted against 1.3 million housing properties, an increase of 79 percent from 2006. Residential and commercial mortgage-related losses suffered by banks and other financial institutions in the United States, the UK, and the eurozone between 2007 and 2010 totaled approximately US$817 billion according to the Global Financial Stability Report April 2010, issued by the International Monetary Fund. A technique known as *securitization* allowed lenders to market mortgage debt to investors through mortgage-backed securities (MBSs) and collateralized debt obligations (CDOs), many of which, incredibly, received AAA ratings from rating agencies who were persuaded by investment banks marketing the securities that the chances of default were low. With those investment-grade ratings, investment banks and insurance companies such as AIA issued credit default swaps (CDS) or insurance policies against the failing CDOs. Hedge funds, seeing the imminent collapse of the housing market aggressively purchased the CDSs. As the value of the mortgage assets fell, investors who held MBSs or CDOs began bailing out and rushing to the safety of U.S. Treasuries. The knock-on effect of this flight to quality led to plummeting stock markets worldwide and bankruptcy for

(*continued*)

(*Continued*)

the banks and insurance companies who had issued CDSs.

Mounting defaults caused lenders to either rein in loans or to raise their interest rates. The accompanying credit crunch prompted central banks in the United States, Japan, and Europe to release funds in order to stimulate financial markets and create a more positive lending climate. The subprime crisis hurt economic growth as both businesses and consumers cut back on spending.

portfolio into pools, which are then sold to investors. To facilitate sales to smaller buyers, the pool is sliced into smaller, more manageable individual units (say, of US$1,000 each), which pay a regular coupon rate. Deducted from the annual coupon rate is a servicing fee. Unlike conventional bonds, MBSs have no fixed maturity date for the return of principal. Mortgage lenders can then use the proceeds from these sales to make new loans to other borrowers. Each pool typically can consist of a variety of different mortgage types of varying maturities and varying ratings.

The payments investors receive consist of both interest and principal on the mortgage. At the beginning, mortgage payments are primarily interest. Over time, this shifts to increasing amounts of principal. Not all borrowers end up paying off their mortgages according to a fixed schedule. If interest rates are trending down, some may decide to prepay their mortgages and refinance their loan. This is referred to as *prepayment risk*, which leads to reinvestment risk—which is another way of saying that bondholders are paid but might not be able to re-invest the money at the same interest rate that they had before. If interest rates rise, the problem of extension risk crops up. During periods of rising interest rates, fewer people prepay their mortgages, and the life of the bond could be extended way beyond what was originally expected.

Mortgage bonds are more sensitive to interest rates shifts than other types of bonds. Prices fall when interest rates are rising and appreciate less when interest rates are falling. The financial term for this is *negative convexity*.

COLLATERALIZED MORTGAGE OBLIGATIONS

A collateralized mortgage obligation (CMO) is a complicated type of mortgage-backed security. Instead of being a mere collection of mortgages, a CMO focuses on specific components. For example, the CMO could be divided up into several maturity classes, or tranches, each with different coupon rates, principal balances, prepayment risks, and maturity dates. Payments are made according to rules that address each maturity class, with schedules that are designed to please investors with different goals.

One investor might want a shorter investment timeframe than the standard 30-year mortgage in exchange for a lower interest rate. Another might want to give up interest payments altogether and invest in *principal-only bonds* via zero-coupon bonds that sell at a discount and repay their full face amount at maturity. This strategy avoids both prepayment risk and reinvestment risk. CMOs are designed with institutional investors in mind. Since they can be highly vulnerable to interest-rate changes and prepayment or refinancing trends, returns from CMOs are often unpredictable.

SUMMARY

Corporate bonds allow companies to raise funds without giving investors an equity stake in the firm. Their perceived stability (regular interest payments and the return of principal) makes them appealing to investors.

Corporate bonds can be classified as secured or unsecured debt. Investors can choose from a wide range of bonds, including convertible bonds, junk bonds, callable and put bonds, international bonds, socially responsible bonds, and more unusual offerings, such as catastrophe bonds.

Mortgage-backed securities are issued by federal agencies, government-sponsored enterprises, and the private sector. The mortgages are packaged into pools, and bondholders receive the monthly interest and principal repayments made by the homeowner.

Collateralized mortgage obligations are more complicated debt instruments that feature more investment choices but are geared mainly to the institutional market. Asset-backed securities are similar to mortgage-backed securities but are collateralized by other kinds of assets, such as credit-card receivables or auto loans.

QUICK QUIZ

1. Why do companies issue corporate bonds?
2. What is the difference between a secured and unsecured corporate bond?
3. What are the attractions of a convertible bond?
4. Define a junk bond.
5. Explain the concept behind a mortgage-backed security.
6. What caused the subprime mortgage crisis?

6

INTERNATIONAL BONDS

International bonds are essentially domestic bonds with one big difference: they are bonds sold internationally and not only to domestic investors in the market where they originated. If a company in Korea issues a bond in Korean won and sells it in the United States, it would be considered an international bond. It could also issue it in U.S. dollars or other currencies, but the fact that the issuer and the buyer are in different countries makes it an international transaction and an international bond. Investors who buy bonds issued outside their home country are able to avail themselves of some very enticing advantages. First, such investments give them an avenue for diversifying investment portfolios and thus reducing volatility or risk. More importantly, international bonds enable the investor to reduce or eliminate taxes. Finally international bonds often offer a higher interest rate than domestic bonds.

Bonds sold internationally have existed for a long time, but it is only in the last 40 years that they have developed into a large and liquid market as a result of the opening of global financial markets and the relaxation or elimination of currency and capital controls. Today, investors are not limited to their home bond market but are able to access a wide range of international bonds. International bonds are given all kinds of names for ease of categorization such as eurobonds, dragon bonds, samurai bonds, and others.

Sometimes bonds are categorized into *developed market bonds* and *emerging market bonds*. In the past this was a way to reflect the perceived higher risk of the emerging market bonds, but in recent years with bond risk defaults rising in developed countries such as Greece, Portugal, Spain, and Ireland, that differentiation may no longer be very relevant.

Nevertheless, problems with emerging market bonds in the past led to a number of structural innovations. Brady bonds, named after former U.S. treasury secretary Nicholas Brady, were created in the late 1980s to stop defaults of emerging countries' debt, particularly in Latin America. In order to give confidence to investors in defaulted Latin American loans, they were collateralized by U.S. Treasury zero-coupon bonds, which ensured that the principal would be repaid. Since the 1980s, when many of the emerging markets suffered from financial turmoil and interest rates on their bonds were very high, those countries have instituted strong fiscal discipline, reduced their debt-to-GDP ratios, and increased their foreign reserves. The result is that interest rates on emerging market bonds have come down.

INTERNATIONAL BOND RISK

Investors who are interested in international bonds should familiarize themselves with three important variables: (1) the creditworthiness of the issuing organization, which is the same procedure that would be followed when examining a domestic bond; (2) the currency in which the bond is issued; and (3) the sovereign risk of the country of origin.

Currency risk refers to the possible devaluation of the currency in which the bond is denominated. Of course, evaluating currency risk requires considering two currencies, the currency in which the bond is issued and the currency of the bond buyer. If you are a U.S. dollar investor and are investing in a Malaysian ringgit bond and the ringgit devalues against the U.S. dollar, then you have lost. However, if you are a euro investor and the ringgit strengthens against the euro, you have a currency gain. Currency changes can be dramatic and can wipe out any interest income or, if the currency moves in the buyer's favor, can result in gains far above any interest gained. A euro investor earning 10 percent interest on a U.S. dollar-denominated bond would gain 19 percent if the U.S. dollar appreciates against the euro by 9 percent over a one-year period. However if the U.S. dollar devalues by 9 percent against the euro during that period the earnings would only be 1 percent over the year.

Sovereign risk refers to the complex political and economic factors that impact a country's stability and most importantly the perception that investors have of that country. If there are civil strife, inflation, military coups, and other such actions, bond investors may get nervous and begin selling the country's bonds, thus pushing prices down resulting in losses to holders of those bonds. Most critical is when governments decide to restrict foreign exchange outflows, even restricting interest payments on bonds or deciding to impose heavy taxes on bond interest payments. Both bonds issued by governments and bonds issued by companies and other organizations could be impacted. Over history, bond defaults have not been uncommon, and even recently defaults occurred in the late 1990s as investors in Russian and Ecuadoran government bonds learned when both those governments defaulted. It is therefore necessary for international bond investors to carefully monitor the political, economic and currency developments of the countries in which they invest. In each country, laws and taxes differ, and they should be understood in light of their possible impact.

TYPES OF INTERNATIONAL BONDS

A number of different names for foreign bonds have been coined to describe bonds depending on their (1) currency, (2) issuing organization, (3) place of issue, and (4) target customers.

CASE STUDY: WHEN DEFAULTS OCCUR

As early as the 1800s, defaults of sovereign bonds occurred mainly related to the downfall of various economies particularly in Latin America as well as some European countries such as Greece, Spain, and Portugal. The defaults in Latin America in the 1890s were caused by concern regarding Argentina's economic stability leading to the collapse of the underwriters, Baring Brothers bank in London. When lending to other Latin American countries was withdrawn by bankers all over the world, six other South American countries defaulted. During the 1930s Great Depression, most European governments defaulted on their debts because of their unsuccessful attempts to remain on the gold standard. Even the British government in 1932 defaulted on its war loan bonds by converting 5 percent bonds into 3.5 percent bonds. Between 1980 and 2004, there were well over 100 defaults, most of which were African and South American government loans. But the most important was Russia's default in 1998 and Argentina's default in 2001, both related to failed exchange rate policies. Most defaults by governments are the result of policies that favor a default on foreign debt rather than an increase in taxes or a reduction in government spending—in other words, political expediency. The so-called debt trap results when a debtor finds that the payments due on a loan are higher than income, and they are forced to borrow more to pay off existing debt.

Here are some of the more common ones but new names and structures are being developed with the market expansion.

Yankee bonds are U.S. dollar-denominated bonds issued to U.S. investors by non-U.S. companies, banks, and foreign governments. They must be registered with the U.S. Securities and Exchange Commission and must comply with the same regulations imposed on U.S. corporations. In recent years, the most common issuers of such bonds have been international banks and corporations. When U.S. interest rates are low, they give foreign issuers an opportunity to benefit from lower interest rates than what they would obtain in their home country. If the issuer has U.S. dollar income from operations in the U.S. or other parts of the world, the currency risk is reduced since interest payments can be made from that U.S. dollar income.

Eurobonds are not necessarily bonds issued in euro currency or by European entities, but are bonds issued in a currency other than the country or market in which the bonds originate. This kind of issuance thus falls outside the regulatory jurisdiction of a single country and thus allows for greater flexibility. For example, a Russian company could issue a U.S. dollar–denominated bond in the London market. Or an Indian company could issue a Japanese yen–denominated bond in Singapore. Eurobonds are normally bearer bonds and thus give the buyers anonymity. In addition there are certain tax advantages. Many people use the term *eurobond* to describe all international bonds.

Dragon bonds are bonds issued in Asian exchanges such as Hong Kong or Singapore and can be in any currency with the U.S. dollar the most popular.

Samurai bonds are denominated in yen, issued by foreign issuers in Japan and subject to Japanese laws.

Sushi bonds are a type of Eurobond issued by a Japanese corporation.

Bulldog bonds are issued in pounds sterling in the UK by a foreign company.

Kangaroo bonds (also known as *Matilda Bonds*) are denominated in Australian dollars and issued in Australia by non-Australian firms.

Maple bonds are denominated in Canadian dollars and sold in Canada by foreign firms.

Panda bonds are denominated in Chinese renminbi and sold in China by non-Chinese institutions.

This is only a partial list of the names given to various types of bonds. We can rely on the creativity of investment bankers and bond originators to come up with more interesting names.

Equity Warrants

In the early 1980s international bonds with equity warrants were first introduced. The extra kicker or benefit of equity warrants meant that issuers could obtain a lower rate of interest by offering the equity warrants as part of the bond issued. The warrants give the holder the right to purchase

NOTE
THE TED SPREAD

The TED spread was named from the initials of "T-Bill" and "ED," the ticker symbol for the eurodollar futures contract. However, the use of eurodollar futures contracts has been replaced with the LIBOR or London Interbank Rate. So now the TED spread indicates the difference in interest rates between three-month U.S. Treasuries and the three-month LIBOR. This spread can be used as a credit-risk indicator since U.S. T-bills are considered risk-free, while the LIBOR rate reflects the credit risk of lending to commercial banks. Therefore, as the TED spread increases, the risk of default is considered to be increasing. A rising TED spread is often used as a predictor of a U.S. stock market downturn as liquidity gets tighter.

shares of the company issuing the bond at a fixed price up to the expiry date. In a rising equity market, such warrants could become quite valuable if the *strike* price is not too much higher than the current share price because if the firm's share price is rising it could develop that the warrant strike price is lower than the market price, thus enabling the holder to make a profit.

INTERNATIONAL BOND MARKET DEVELOPMENT

The international bond market actually started to be significant from the 1820s when foreign bond issuers, mostly governments and railway companies, were active in the London financial market. From that time to World War I, London and Paris were the main financial centers for foreign bond trading and issuance. London and Paris then lost their preeminence because of the imposition of exchange controls in those markets along with other problems. New York then became the main center for foreign bonds after World War II with U.S. dollar Yankee bonds predominating. During the 1980s Japanese yen and Swiss franc bonds issues expanded rapidly.

Eurobonds were first developed in the 1960s and grew rapidly after that. Originally U.S. dollar–denominated bonds were most popular because of the accumulation of offshore dollar balances during the late 1950s and early 1960s. There was a fear that dollar accounts held in the United States might be frozen, so investors wanted to trade and hold the U.S. dollar bonds offshore. Borrowers thus bypassed the U.S. capital market's ratings and disclosure requirements and sold directly to European investors. The weakening of the Bretton Woods system during the 1960s and the flow of gold from the U.S. Federal Reserve to other central banks indicated a deteriorating U.S. external position. In addition, the introduction in the U.S.

Regulation Q fixing a maximum rate of interest—which during the 1940s and 1950s was set at or below 3 percent—for deposits in U.S. banks resulted in the movement of deposits and bond issuance to foreign banks who offered higher U.S. dollar interest rates.

In 1963, the U.S. government then tried to limit the outflow of USD by introducing an Interest Equalization Tax designed to raise the effective annual cost to foreigners borrowing in the United States by 1 percent. The result was that European borrowers curtailed their use of the Yankee bond market and instead moved to the new eurobond market. Later, U.S. government restrictions discouraged U.S. banks from lending to U.S. corporations for their overseas operations; therefore many U.S. multinational companies moved to the eurobond market as the only available source of long-term credit for their overseas operations.

By the end of the 1960s, a thriving market for eurobonds, including deutsche mark bonds developed because of the German government's desire to take pressure off the strengthening deutsche mark, German investors were encouraged to purchase foreign bonds since they would result in capital outflow and ease upward pressure on the currency. They also wanted to discourage the acquisition of domestic German bonds by foreigners, so, again, the eurobond issuance was encouraged.

As the market for U.S. dollar–denominated eurobonds expanded, bonds in other currencies such as French francs and Canadian dollars were introduced. The market expanded rapidly because of increased financial liberalization not only in Europe but in the UK and Japan. Also a very active secondary market in the bonds developed in London, which facilitated growth of the market. In addition, the growth of the swap market further encouraged market development.

Probably the most critical factor that has favored the development of eurobonds is that they do not need to be registered with the U.S. Securities and Exchange Commission (SEC) and thus avoid the plethora or regulations imposed by U.S. law. Also, in capital markets of a number of countries, domestic bonds are subject to withholding tax, while international bonds denominated in the domestic currency typically are not. So there are regulatory as well as tax advantages.

TRADING AND SETTLEMENT

Clearing Houses

Trading of international bonds takes place in exchanges all over the world. In order to ensure proper and fair settlement of bond transactions, buyers and sellers rely on international clearing houses, which are separate independent agencies or corporations responsible for ensuring that both sides of the transaction are completed fairly and efficiently.

Clearstream is one such major clearing house. Formerly known as Cedel, it was founded in 1971 and was owned by 92 banks. In July 2002, it became a division of the Deutsche Börse and became known as Clearstream.

Another major bond clearing system, and reputedly the world's largest, is Euroclear. In addition to settling domestic bond and international bond transactions, it also settles equities, derivatives, and investment funds. It now provides securities services to financial institutions located in more than 90 countries. Euroclear also acts as an international securities depository, the Central Securities Depository (CSD), for Belgian, Dutch, Finnish, French, Irish, Swedish, and UK securities. It is based in Brussels, Belgium, was founded in 1968 by J.P. Morgan & Co. and operated by the Morgan subsidiary Morgan Guaranty Trust Company of New York. In 2001, Morgan Guaranty transferred all activities to Euroclear Bank, which is owned by the market participants using its services, mostly banks and broker-dealers.

Trading Patterns

Bond prices tend to follow a sawtooth pattern rising right before an interest payment is to be made and falling after the payment is made. In order to eliminate the sawtooth pattern, price quotations are usually *clean* and are made up of the clean price plus an item termed *accrued interest*, which is directly proportional to the time that has elapsed since the last dividend payment. The interest accrued between two dates in the same coupon period is calculated according to the formula:

$$AI = (d \times G)/Ay$$

where AI = accrued interest
d = number of days between the two dates
G = coupon rate
Ay = assumed number of days in a year

It should be kept in mind that there are different definitions used for the above terms in various markets. For example, for "Ay" sometimes the assumption is a 365-day year while at other times it could be 360 days. For eurobonds, the accrued interest is normally calculated on a 30-day month and a 360-day year. Settlement dates of bond transactions vary from a few business days to as much as a week.

TAXES AND BEARER STATUS

Most international bonds, and in particular nearly all eurobonds, come in bearer form with the certificates usually with a nominal value of about $1,000. The bonds themselves consist of certificates usually with a nominal value of around $1,000. Attached to the bonds is a set of detachable coupon slips, one for each coupon payment. When the coupon is presented on the appropriate date, the paying agent (normally a bank) makes the payment.

Bearer bond ownership is indicated simply by whoever is in possession of the certificate. In the 1960s when Eurobond trading grew, this presented problems since there were many instances of failed delivery of the physical certificates. Investors and traders simply did not present their bonds or coupons on time. There was thus a move to *book entry* systems to substitute the physical movement of bond paper. The book entry system tracks ownership of securities when there is no certificate issued or where a *master certificate* representing all certificates is kept permanently in a safe. Where there are *book-entry-only* (BEO) issues, investors do not receive certificates, but the custodian holds one or more global certificates. There are also *dematerialized securities*, where no certificates exist and the security issuer keeps records, usually electronically, of who holds the outstanding securities).

The convenience of book entry systems means that most investors will opt for that system, so that the investor's broker will have the bonds held in book entry form. This obviates the need for moving certificates around when buying and selling takes place, as well as avoiding replacement costs in cases of certificate damage or loss.

The establishment of the clearing houses, as mentioned, facilitated this change so that the securities are registered in the computer systems of the clearing houses on behalf of banks and trading houses acting on behalf of clients.

The exemption from taxes is a significant advantage for the international bonds, since many governments charge tax on interest earned as well as capital gains. In cases where taxes might be charged, it has been the practice to register bonds in shell companies in tax havens such as the Netherlands Antilles.

ISSUING AND UNDERWRITING

International bonds are issued by banks, or syndicates of banks, on behalf of borrowers, whether they be a company or a country. At the first stage, the borrower works with the managing or underwriting bank or bank group to design the bond structure and conditions. After completion of the prospectus detailing all aspects of the transaction, the bond issue is initiated with the underwriting group taking possession of the bond. Prior to that time, the underwriters will have contact with a selling group of dealers or brokers in addition to important bond customers to get a sense of the market and even to presell the bond issue. Since the underwriters assume the financial risk, they have a big enough discount to enable them to make a profit when they resell the bonds. There is always a risk that market interest rates will change between the time when the underwriter has purchased the bonds and the time when they are resold, resulting in a loss for the underwriter. Also the selling group will have been asked to participate and help sell the bonds although they would not be liable for any unsold bonds. The bonds are sold at a discount to the selling group who then sell at a higher price to obtain a profit.

Investment banks are most active in underwriting. Since they advise companies on mergers, acquisitions, currency trading, derivatives, and a host of other transactions, they are well qualified to understand the financial requirements of the companies they advise and thus are able to structure bond offerings that will satisfy both the borrowers and the bond buyers.

Bond sales can take place by competitive bidding or by negotiated sales or private placements. In all these kinds of sales, the underwriters work closely with traders and sales persons to determine the price of a new issue. In private placements, issuers may sell the bonds directly to investors or through a placement agent who acts as an intermediary between the bond issuer and the bond investors. Investment banks are the most common placement agents who are in contact with institutional investors, such as pension funds, insurance companies, trust funds, endowments, sovereign wealth funds, and high-net-worth individuals. When acting as a placement agent, the banks will most commonly be compensated with a fee.

Where there is a competitive sale (also called an advertised sale or sealed bid sale), various underwriters will submit sealed bids to purchase the bonds from the issuer. The underwriting bidder offering the lowest interest cost to the issuer will then be awarded the bid, and that bid becomes the sales contract for the offering. The underwriter or syndicate of underwriters then purchases the bonds and resells them to other investors or a selling group.

In a negotiated bond sale, the organization issuing the bonds selects the underwriter, or syndicate of underwriters, by first sending out a Request for Proposal (RFP) specifying the selection criteria. After all proposals are received from the banks, one or a group is selected as the underwriter or syndicate of underwriters. The selected underwriter(s) then have the exclusive right to purchase the bonds at a specified price. A lead underwriter or manager is chosen to coordinate the issue and sets a preliminary pricing schedule that may be revised upward or downward until a final price is reached on the sale date.

NOTE
BEFORE THERE WERE RULEMAKERS

In the government and municipal bond market, competition can be fierce among bankers wishing to do a deal, with the result that "pay to play" scandals occur. Political contributions and influence peddling involving top executives of securities firms attempting to get bond-issuing mandates became common. In the United States in the early 1990s, a group of Wall Street firms representing 75 percent of the municipal underwriting business, called for a voluntary ban on political contributions by their municipal bond departments. Before the municipal market's self-regulatory body, the Municipal Securities Rulemaking Board (MSRB), the firms proposed a rule to limit business-related contributions by Wall Street banks and brokers.

In a private placement, there is a direct transaction between the issuer and investors without an underwriter. In such cases, placement agents act as intermediaries between the issuer and investors but do not assume any underwriting risks. Sometimes, issuers may do away with a placement agent and deal directly with the ultimate investor in what is called a direct purchase.

When there is competitive bidding and a selling group, it is difficult to impose uniform pricing since various members of the selling group may offer discounts, even though the lead manager wants to impose the same price for all buyers. Therefore, immediately after the issue is sold the manager or managing group tries to stabilize prices by buying and selling the bonds on the market.

Bought deals are bond launches in which the buyers are already fixed at the time of the issue and where the bond houses bid on a fixed-price basis with all the terms and conditions fixed as well and not subject to alteration. This method has advantages for the borrower since he knows what the cost of funds will be and the deal will not be subject to market movements. Also a bought deal can be made quickly, which enables the borrower to take advantage of temporary market conditions.

SWAPS

The issuing of international bonds has been facilitated by the development of swaps, both currency swaps and interest rate swaps. A U.S. dollar investor may not want to take the currency risk of a Japanese yen-denominated issue even though he is attracted to the other terms and conditions. In such a case, the investor can swap the yen value of a bond for U.S. dollars at the time of purchase and maintain that swap for as long as he holds the bond.

An interest rate swap can protect an investor who is offered a variable interest rate bond but is afraid that interest rates will go down. He can then swap the variable interest rate feature for a fixed rate.

Currency swaps are essentially an agreement between two parties to exchange the principal or interest payments (or both) of a bond or loan in one currency for another currency. They were originally conceived in the 1970s to avoid United Kingdom foreign exchange controls. Because of those controls at that time, British companies had to pay a premium to borrow U.S. dollars. To avoid these premiums, companies established back-to-back loan agreements with U.S. companies wanting to borrow pounds sterling. During the 2008 subprime crisis the U.S. Federal Reserve used currency swaps to exchange domestic currencies of various countries at the prevailing exchange rates and agreed to reverse those swaps at the same rates at future dates in order to provide liquidity in U.S. dollars to overseas markets.

There are a number of ways such swaps can work. In the simplest case, only the principal is swapped at an agreed exchange rate, which would be applied at a specific future date. Another method is where the swap combines both the principal of the bond as well as the interest. Another variation is to swap only the interest payment cash flows, where the payments are converted to the negotiated currency from the original currency.

Interest rate swaps are normally used to exchange fixed-interest payments or variable-rate interest payments. If an investor has purchased a variable–interest rate bond and thinks interest rates are going up, he can trade the variable rate cash flows with an investor with a fixed-rate bond who thinks interest rates are going up. The net result is that each party swaps their existing cash flows. There is no exchange of the principal amounts but only the interest payments.

In most cases such swaps, whether they be currency or interest rates, are arranged by banks who match the parties and transactions taking a percent or *spread* from the swap payments. Since such swaps are over-the-counter (OTC), there is great variation, and deals can be structured to meet the special needs of the counterparties.

The market for such swaps has grown dramatically and attracted speculators, which has increased liquidity. The notional amount outstanding of such swaps is now estimated to be in excess of $350 trillion.

CASE STUDY: THE INTERNATIONAL SWAPS AND DERIVATIVES ASSOCIATION

The International Swaps and Derivatives Association (ISDA) was formerly called the International Swap Dealers Association. It is a New York–based organization with a membership of over 800 in more than 50 countries, including dealers, bankers, and others involved in the over-the-counter derivatives market. In addition to establishing a standardized Master Agreement for derivatives transactions between a derivatives dealers and counterparties, the organization manages computer language standards and is involved in generally promoting and policing its industry. The ISDA Master Agreement standardized contract for derivatives transactions serves the critical function of allowing the parties to a transaction to aggregate the amounts owed to each and have a single net amount payable to one part of another. In time of turmoil in the markets, the agreement allows for assessment of amounts to be paid to each party.

CREDIT DEFAULT SWAPS (CDS)

A CDS is, in fact, a kind of insurance policy. If an investor wants to ensure against a default on the bonds he holds, he purchase a CDS. This is essentially a transfer of the credit exposure or risk from one investor to another. The investor accepting the risk is paid the CDS price. CDS prices are a useful indicator of the risk perception of investors. If investors think a particular bond is risky, the CDS prices move up.

SECONDARY MARKET

Trading in the bond secondary market includes dealers (mostly banks) and a small number of interdealer brokers (IDBs). The IDBs first came into being in the late 1970s to act as an intermediary between various deals, so that the dealers could deal anonymously with each other. When a dealer wants to sell or buy a bond, he contacts the IDB who registers the offer without the name of the offering deal on its electronic trading screen. The screen is available to other dealers who then can register their interest to trade. Normally, the screens are available only to reporting dealers who are members of the Association of International Bond Dealers (AIBD) a self-regulated association of dealers in eurobonds. Formed in 1969 with its head office in Zurich, Switzerland, it was established to set standards for trading and settlement in the international bond market. Among other activities, the AIBD monitors interdealer brokers to ensure that rules are being followed. The Association also publishes bond price lists, which have become the key sources for international bond prices. This is particularly important since a large number of bonds are not liquid, so with a limited secondary market it is difficult to assess bond prices for preparing financial statements for bond holders.

The clearing houses have introduced bond lending facilities for those traders who wish to short sell bonds and for institutions that hold bonds long term and are willing to get paid for lending the bonds. The amount of borrowing is relatively small, since the clearing houses put limits on the amount of any bond lending.

SUMMARY

International bonds are bonds not only sold to domestic investors in the country where the bond originated but to investors all over the world. Although such bonds have existed for a very long time, it is only in the last 40 years that they have represented a large and liquid market. The key risks for international bonds are currency risk and sovereign risk. New forms and structures for international bonds continue to be created however, the most well-known types include: Yankee bonds, eurobonds, dragon bonds, samurai bonds, sushi bonds, bulldog bonds, kangaroo bonds, maple bonds, and panda bonds. Trading of international bonds takes place all over the world, but one critical function consists of the bonds clearing and settlement systems that are now dominated by a few major firms such as Clearstream and Euroclear. International bond issues depend on potential tax liabilities as well as the availability of currency and interest rate swaps. The secondary market for international bonds is facilitated by bank bond dealers and inter-dealer brokers.

QUICK QUIZ

1. What were Brady bonds, and why were they created?
2. Can defaults of bonds issued by governments occur? Why?
3. What are eurobonds? Why are they favored?
4. What is the TED spread?
5. What is the use of currency swaps? Why are they used?
6. How about interest rate swaps? What are they, and how are they used?

7

BOND CALCULATIONS

Many investors find calculating bond rates, yields, and returns quite intimidating if they are not particularly fond of math. Actually, bond mathematics need not be intimidating since the tools for calculations are easily available. In fact, the Internet has come to the rescue. On any number of websites, all that is required is to input a few numbers into blank fields, and the freely available calculators enable you to input the variables of any bond and then calculate everything, from current yield on coupon income and yield to maturity, to figuring out taxable yield equivalents and the performance of tax-exempt bonds vis-à-vis taxable bonds, and so on.

In this chapter, we'll examine the background and structure of bond mathematics to provide a basic understanding of the terms used, what the figures mean, and how they can affect investment decisions.

PAR

Bonds are issued at different face values—$1,000, $5,000, $25,000, or more. The face or *par* value is the principal that will be returned when the bonds mature. A statement such as "This bond is valued at par" simply means that the bond's current price or value is the same as the original face value, whatever that may have been. A statement such as "The bond is valued at 95" means the bond is now selling at 95 percent of its par value. Thus, if the face value is $1,000, then selling at 95 would mean a price of $950. If the face value is $10,000, the price at 95 would be $9,500.

BID/ASK

All bonds have a *bid* price and an *ask* price. The bid price is the price offer made by a bond buyer. In a table of bid/ask prices, it is normally shown on the left side column. The ask price, or the price offered by bond sellers, is normally shown on the right. A hypothetical bid price might be 102, and the ask price 102¼. When a bank or broker is listing prices, the bid price, of course, will always be lower than the ask price since the buyers want to buy at a lower price than the seller is willing to sell. Since bond dealers or traders are in the middle of the trade between sellers and buyers, the difference between the bid and ask prices is the *spread*—the profit that dealers/traders can make by buying and selling bonds.

What do these prices mean? Initially bonds would normally be sold at the par value. U.S. dollar bonds are normally sold in units of a par value of US$1,000. Once the bonds are quoted on the market, the price would veer away from the par value and be quoted in a percentage of the original par value. For example, a bid price of 102 represents 102 percent of par value, so that for a bond with a par value of US$1,000, the bid value would be US$1,020, while an ask price might be 102¼ or a value of $1,022.50. The $2.50 difference is the *spread*.

BASIS POINTS

A *basis point* equals 1/100th of a percent or 0.01 percent. Thus, 100 basis points equal 1 percent. When bond traders talk about the yield increasing from 2 percent to 2.5 percent, they will often say that the yield has increased by 50 basis points. If the yield has gone from 2 percent to 3 percent, then they would say that it has increased by 100 basis points. The use of basis points helps eliminate confusion over changes in yields as opposed to percentage changes. For example, if the yield on a bond increases from 4 percent to 5 percent, this could be described in two ways: as a 1 percent increase (5 percent minus 4 percent) in yield or as a percentage change of 25 percent (1/4 = 0.25 or 25 percent). Saying that the yield has increased by 100 basis points helps clarify matters.

PREMIUM AND DISCOUNT BONDS

If a bond's bid or ask price is above 100—that is, it is worth more than its par value—it is a *premium bond*. Conversely, a bond quoted at less than 100 is worth less than its par value and is known as a *discount bond*. As we have noted, there is an inverse relationship between bond prices and prevailing market interest rates. If market interest rates rise, a fixed-interest bond's value will fall. Premium and discount bonds represent deviations from par as a result of increases or decreases in market interest rates.

A premium bond indicates that interest rates have fallen and that you're lucky enough to be holding a bond that pays interest higher than market rates. For example, your bond is paying 5 percent interest, and market interest rates have declined to 4 percent. The price of a bond should reflect that the bond's 5 percent interest is paying 1 percent more interest than the prevailing market interest rate of 4 percent. The bond price thus rises to an amount above par, so that the extra 1 percent interest is accounted for. (*Note:* In these examples we are dealing with fixed-interest bonds and not bonds that adjust their interest to changes in inflation or prevailing interest rates.)

For example, if market rates are 4 percent and a $1,000 bond is paying an interest of 5 percent, that bond's price will be higher than $1,000 to reflect that difference in interest rates. If market interest rates fall to 2 percent, the bond becomes even more valuable, and its price rises higher.

A discount bond works the same way in reverse. Suppose the same $1,000 bond pays a coupon rate of 3 percent, but market interest rates have increased to 4 percent. The holder of a bond paying only 3 percent in this interest rate environment might be feeling a little disappointed. If he wanted to sell the bond, the only way to generate sufficient interest among traders would be to lower the bond's price enough so that the new price exactly offsets the 1 percent difference in interest rates.

ACCRUED INTEREST

Another concept involving bond calculations is related to *accrued interest*. Although bond interest payments are made on a quarterly, half yearly, or yearly basis, interest is calculated daily. This is important if a bond is to be sold, since the buyer price should include the accrued interest up to the day the bond ownership changes hands. When a bond is purchased, accrued interest is incorporated into the price. For instance, if a bond for which interest is paid every six months is sold four months after the interest was last paid, the seller is entitled to receive the accrued interest. Thus, the buyer pays the sale price, plus four months' interest to the seller. So it is calculated as the annual interest amount multiplied by the number of days that four months represents divided by 360 days of the year.

Calculating accrued interest on a zero-coupon bond requires a different approach. Instead of making a coupon interest payment every six months, zeros are issued at a discount from their principal value to make up for the interest not paid. So assume that a $5,000 zero-coupon bond yielding 4 percent matures in seven years. To find out the issue price of this zero, its *present value* must first be determined. This can be accomplished by using a bond calculation, which includes the value at maturity, the interest rate, and the time. So our handy bond calculators will tell us that the bond's issue price or *present value* at issue is $3,799. Over seven years, interest would accrue and be automatically reinvested (with all the benefits of compounding) until the bond reached its full $5,000 maturity value. To figure out how much interest would be earned each day (and thus how much the bond's price would rise), take the difference between the maturity value and the issue price ($5,000 − $3,799 = $1,201) and divide that by the number of days until the bond matures (7 × 365 = 2,555). (To make things simpler, leap years have been excluded.) So, 1,201/2,555 = 0.47 cents. The bond's par value would increase in value by 47 cents each day, assuming that market interest rates remain constant, which is unlikely. However, the method serves as a useful guide to the increments in a zero coupon's value over the life of the bond.

CLEAN PRICE VERSUS DIRTY PRICE

Two terms used when referring to accrued interest are clean price and dirty price:

Clean Price: This is the price of a coupon bond not including accrued interest. It gives the discounted future cash flows without any accruing interest in the next coupon payment date. Immediately following each coupon payment, the clean price becomes equal to the *dirty price*.

Dirty Price: This is the price including the present value of all future cash flows with interest accruing on the next coupon payment.

BOND EQUIVALENT YIELD

For fixed-income securities that mature in less than one year, calculating the bond equivalent yield (BEY) converts the simple interest rates for semiannual, quarterly, or monthly notes into an annual yield. This allows securities with shorter maturities to be accurately compared with securities that have an annual yield. The BEY is also known as the investment rate or equivalent coupon yield. For a \$1,000 bond, the calculation would be to subtract the purchase price from the \$1,000 par, divide by the purchase price, and multiply by 365 days divided by the days to maturity as follows:

$$\frac{\$1{,}000 - \text{Purchase Price}}{\text{Purchase Price}} \times \frac{365}{\text{Days to Maturity}}$$

TYPES OF BOND YIELDS

Bond returns are based on five kinds of yield

1. Coupon yield
2. Current yield
3. Yield to maturity
4. Yield to call
5. Yield to worst

Coupon Yield

The coupon yield is the nominal rate the bond issuer has promised to pay for the life of the bond and is the easiest to calculate. If a \$1,000 bond is paying a 5 percent coupon rate annually, the investor receives \$50 in income (5 percent × \$1,000 = \$50). If the coupon is paid semiannually, the amount will be \$25, twice a year throughout the life of the bond.

Current Yield

The current yield is used to determine the yield on a bond whose price has changed from its par value. It is calculated by dividing the bond's coupon yield by its market price to give the annual return on the price paid for the bond. For example, for a 10-year $1,000 par value bond paying a coupon yield of 5 percent that is selling for $950, the current yield is calculated by dividing the annual coupon payments by the bond price $950. A 5 percent yield equals to $50 which divided by the bond price of $950 comes to 5.26 percent (50/950), which is the current yield. It is a higher percent than the coupon yield because the bond price has come down making it a discount bond. If this were a premium bond selling for $1,050, the current yield would be lower at 4.76 percent ($50 divided by $1,050).

Although current yield can provide a useful snapshot of returns at a given time, it changes as often as the bond's price does.

Yield to Maturity (YTM)

Yield to maturity is the classic yield measurement and is often defined as the average rate of return that a bond earns if it is bought and held to maturity. YTM takes into consideration (1) the principal, (2) the amount of interest earned from the time the bond was purchased until maturity, plus (3) any capital gain (premium bond) or loss (discount bond). It assumes that interest payments are reinvested and earning compound interest at the same coupon rate that the bond is paying. This may not necessarily be true, but for purposes of calculation those assumption are made.

For example, a bond calculator may show that the YTM on a 10-year, $1,000 par-value bond bought for $950 with a coupon rate of 5 percent is 5.67 percent. In addition, the YTM on a discount bond will always be higher than the current yield because the YTM takes into account the $1,000 principal that will be returned at maturity—the extra $50 adds to the profit. On premium bonds, the YTM will be less than the current yield because the par value is below the price paid for the bond.

Yield-to-Call and Yield-to-Worst

Yield to maturity assumes that the bond will be held to maturity. This is not always the case with callable bonds, which can be redeemed by the issuer before maturity. In this situation, the *yield-to-call* replaces YTM. Bonds are more likely to be called when market interest rates are falling (making premium bonds most vulnerable to calls) for the simple reason that it's more cost effective for companies to refinance the bond at lower coupon rates than to continue paying higher ones. This puts bondholders in a less-than-advantageous position because not only have they lost their higher coupon rates, they are also faced with lower market interest rates when they reinvest their future coupon income stream.

Another term, *yield-to-worst*, refers to a bond with a variety of call dates and prices. This considers all the redemption possibilities and gives the yield that is the poorest of all possible yields to call. This enables the bondholder to brace for the worst-case scenario.

TOTAL RETURN

The concept of total return looks at the amount of money that can be made over a particular investment period. Unlike YTM, which assumes that the buyer will keep the bond until maturity, total return can cover a shorter period of time and gives the return for the time period when the bond is held. This is useful for investors who buy and sell bonds before they mature. The coupon rate and a bond's capital gain or loss are two of the main elements in calculating total return. A third, and perhaps the most important, is the reinvestment rate on the coupon income—especially on a long-term bond. The amount of compound interest earned on reinvested coupon payments can easily dwarf the principal over time. If, for example, a semiannual coupon of $25 on a 20-year 5 percent $1,000 bond is reinvested at the same 5 percent annual rate each time a payment is made, at the end of 20 years the bond would be worth $2,685.06. The returned principal accounts for $1,000, while the reinvested coupons total $1,685.06. Note, though, that the reinvestment rate could be higher or lower.

But suppose an investor wants to sell the bond before it matures, in four years' time, for example. To do this, he will need to consider three factors: the coupon interest over the four years, the reinvested interest over the same period, and the expected price of the bond after four years.

THE IMPACT OF INFLATION

Fixed-income investors must always remain acutely aware of inflation because of its power to erode bonds' total return. Inflation, of course, occurs when the general level of prices for goods and services rises, with the result that purchasing power decreases. If inflation is running at 3 percent a year, an item that costs $1 today will cost $1.03 at the end of the year. The same 3 percent rate of inflation will push the price of a $200,000 home to $206,000 over the same period.

When calculating total return, it's important to weigh the effects of inflation. If inflation is 3 percent and the bond rate of return is 5 percent, the investor's real rate of return is roughly the difference between the two or, in this case, about 2 percent. To obtain a more precise figure, the impact of inflation eroding both the principal and any gains that have been made must be considered. So the real rate of return will be less than 2 percent.

Inflation is anathema to bondholders of fixed-interest bonds because fixed-coupon payments may extend 10, 20, or 30 years into the future, and bonds have no provision for cost-of-living adjustments. Rising inflation also generally leads to higher interest rates, which makes bonds with lower interest rates less desirable and puts downward pressure on bond prices (discount bonds).

Taxation is another factor that can hurt an investor's return. Tax-sheltered municipal bonds can offer an escape route from taxes because these are exempt from federal taxes and, in some cases, from state taxes.

BONDS AND INTEREST RATES

As has been pointed out earlier, interest-rate movements have an enormous effect on bond prices. When interest rates fall, bond prices rise. When interest rates increase, bond prices decline. In each case, the bond price must be adjusted to compensate for the higher or lower rate.

If economic conditions are robust and businesses need money to expand their operations, rates are likely to rise. In a stagnant economy where businesses feel less inclined to borrow money, rates are likely to fall because of lower demand.

Central banks in countries around the world, including the U.S. Federal Reserve Board, have the power to raise or lower interest rates and expand or contract the money supply in order to maintain a healthy economic balance between the need for, and availability of, credit.

The central banks typically act in response to various stages of the business cycle (recovery, expansion, peak, contraction, and recession). During the recession and recovery stages, money supply increases to generate business growth. As the economy responds, the Fed is likely to tighten credit if there are signs of overheating. At the peak stage, inflation becomes a concern, and the Fed may raise short-term interest rates to cool things off. Business contraction follows, with the economy bottoming out with the arrival of a recession.

Often, the best times to buy bonds are during a recession, when bond prices are low and yields are high, and in the recovery stage, when both high yields and capital appreciation make bonds attractive. During economic expansion as interest rates are trending higher, the prices of short-term and intermediate-term bonds weaken as yields increase. Prices continue to fall during the contraction stage as business conditions worsen.

DURATION

Duration is a technical term used in bond analysis to describe how the price of a bond changes as a result of interest rate changes. Frederick Macaulay, an economist who lived between 1882 and 1970, introduced the concept of bond duration and developed a mathematical formula to measure the effective maturity of a bond and the sensitivity of its price to changes in interest rates. The formula took each of the bond coupon payments and computed their weighted average payment time. The formula enables the analyst to calculate the time needed to recover both interest and principal in present-value terms. When comparing two bonds, calculating duration makes it easier to tell which one to buy if each has a different coupon rate and a different original maturity date.

The related concept of *modified duration* is more appealing to bond industry participants since it is a simpler and more practical tool to use. The modified duration formula uses the McCaulay's Duration numbers and determines the impact that a 100-basis-point (1 percent) change in interest rates will have on the price of a bond.

CONVEXITY

Convexity is another concept used by bond analysts. As interest rates change, the price is not likely to change linearly or in a straight line, but instead it is likely to change over some curved function of interest rates. The more curved the price function of the bond is, the more inaccurate duration is as a measure of the interest rate sensitivity. In actual markets, the assumption of constant and even interest rates changes is not correct. Therefore, more complex models are needed to actually price bonds. Therefore, the graphic representation of a bond's price/yield relationship is a convex curve rather than a straight line. Generally, higher convexity will indicate that the bond price will be more sensitive to decreasing interest rates and less sensitive to increasing interest rates. Two bonds with the same coupon, same maturity, and same par value could have different convexities depending on where on the price/yield curve they are located.

SUMMARY

Understanding the mathematics of bonds is extremely useful for successful investing. The concept is more important than the mechanics, thanks to the availability of bond calculator websites. Mastering the basics, such as par and the difference between a premium and discount bond, paves the way toward an understanding of the more sophisticated aspects of bond investing.

Knowledgeable investors should know how to calculate the amount of interest earned between coupon payments (accrued interest) and the bond equivalent yield, which converts simple interest rates on shorter-term bonds into an annual yield.

All investors want to know how much of a return they are making on their money. In calculating this, coupon yield, current yield, yield to maturity, and total return are essential for determining a bond's value. Inflation and the tax implications of bond returns also have to be factored in.

Potential investors would also do well to have some understanding of the relationship between bonds and interest rates as well as more advanced investment concepts such as duration, bond convexity, and standard deviation.

QUICK QUIZ

1. Explain how bond prices are quoted in bond tables.
2. What is the difference between calculating the accrued interest on a coupon-paying bond and a zero-coupon bond?
3. What impact does coupon income have on a bond's total return?

8 RISK

Risk is everywhere, and no one can escape it. We face risk from the day we are born until the day we die. The unexpected can happen at any moment. The tsunamis and earthquakes that have hit various parts of the world are often unexpected and a surprise to people who think that they are safe. Risk is, of course, prevalent in the investment world, and fixed-income instruments are no exception. It can truly be said that there are no risk-free investments. Even what looks like a solid blue chip government or company bond with triple A ratings can be hit with events that render the issuers unable to pay their debts. Companies go bust, and even government goes bust. Walter Wriston, former chairman of Citibank, once declared that "Countries don't go bust." But actually a number of governments over the years have been unable or unwilling to pay bonds that they issued.

Some believe that any bonds issued in a country's domestic currency are risk-free since the government can always print money to pay back the bonds. However, governments have been known to renege on their promises, as Russia did in August 1998 (see Case Study, following), as increasing the money supply leads to greater risk of inflation, which in turn depreciates the local currency and reduces the buying power of investments. So, all bonds or fixed-income investments must be viewed as having varying degrees of risk.

RISK AND RETURN

When planning for risk, there are two very important elements: First, the risk must be recognized by careful research. Next, the risk must be rewarded. There is no sense in taking a risk unless there is the possibility of a commensurate reward. Thus, there is always a trade-off between the degree of risk and the degree of returns. A bond with a greater degree of risk would not be accepted by investors unless the interest rate paid was higher, the price of the bond was expected to appreciate, or the currency in which the bond was denominated was expected to strengthen against the investors' home currency.

Some investors think that bonds or other fixed-income investments are typically less volatile than stocks, but this is not the case since bond prices

CASE STUDY: FINANCIAL CRISES IN ASIA AND RUSSIA

Foreign-currency valuations can ride the rollercoaster of a country's political situation, monetary policy, and economic conditions. The Asian financial crisis of 1997–1998 was touched off when the Thai government failed to defend the Thai baht against international speculators. The baht quickly lost more than half its value, and the financial crisis swiftly spread throughout Southeast Asia.

The crisis led to slumping stock markets, falling currencies, and devaluations in asset prices as well as increases in private debt. Devaluations in asset prices led to defaults on bonds. Credit began to dry up, and bankruptcies climbed, worsening the crisis. In addition to Thailand, Indonesia and South Korea were among the hardest hit, with Hong Kong, Malaysia, Laos, and the Philippines affected to a lesser extent.

Although the Asian financial crisis swept through economies like a virus, it was over in a relatively short period of time. However, the repercussions for developing countries went far beyond the region. The economic slowdown it spawned caused oil prices to tumble, to as low as US$8 a barrel at one point. Russia's loss of US$4 billion in oil revenues in 1998 was a contributing factor in the Russian financial crisis of 1998.

As with the Asian financial crisis, currency vulnerability was at the heart of the debacle that led Russia to default on its bonds, devalue its currency, and suspend payments by commercial banks to foreign creditors.

In November 1997, the country had weathered the first of several speculative attacks on its currency. By December of that year, prices of oil and nonferrous metals began to fall. A second attack against the ruble was launched in April 1998. As concerns about Russia's economic stability began to mount, major investors began disposing of their securities and government bond portfolios. By May, government bond yields had jumped to 47 percent (inflation was running at 10 percent at the time), but nervousness about repayment meant there were few buyers. The accompanying paucity of cash in the system made it hard for commercial banks and firms to remain solvent. In June, the Central Bank of Russia once again rose to defend the ruble, spending US$5 billion in reserves.

On August 13, 1998, investors' fears about a devaluation in the ruble and defaults on domestic debt resulted in the collapse

(*continued*)

(*Continued*)

of Russia's stock, bond, and currency markets. About US$40 billion in bonds were affected. Ultimately, the ruble's fixed peg to the U.S. dollar was abandoned and the currency devalued. The devaluation actually worked to the advantage of domestic Russian industries by making imports more expensive. Although the crisis caused Russia's gross domestic product to decline 4.9 percent in 1998, the country was able to rebound fairly quickly, due to rising oil prices after mid-1999.

can be as volatile as stocks and commodities. Even highly rated investment-grade bonds have been known to fall victim to speculation if, for example, a company's financial condition changes drastically or for a host of other reasons.

TYPES OF RISK

Bond investors face many risks, and it is important for us to delve into each of these, as set out below.

Interest-Rate Risk

There is an inverse relationship between interest rates and bond prices. When interest rates fall, bond prices rise. When bond prices fall, it is an indication that interest rates are rising. For example, if an investor owns a bond with a yield of 3 percent and the prevailing interest rates in the market rise to 5 percent, that 3 percent bond will fall in price because people holding it will want to sell in order to get the 5 percent rate. Of course, buyers of the 3 percent bond will be scarce since they can get the higher 5 percent rate. The opposite will happen if prevailing interest rates fall to, say, 1 percent. At that point the 3 percent bond price will rise as investors will want to get the higher rate.

Market interest rates change constantly because of varying credit conditions. As we have seen, interest rates and bond prices always move in opposite directions. When a bond's coupon is fixed and does not change when market rates rise or fall, adjusting the bond's price (face value) is the only way to adjust for the higher or lower market rate. But if the bond is held until maturity and not traded, interest-rate risk is not a factor because bondholders receive the full amount of their principal.

The longer the bond's term, the more its price will fluctuate with interest-rate changes. With a long-term bond, the potential losses or gains accumulate over the years. This includes reinvestment risks. Therefore, the price of the bond must take all of the bond's remaining years to maturity into account.

In the face of interest-rate volatility, bonds with larger coupons could fare better than those with smaller coupons, which are more prone to being relegated to discount-bond status if the interest rate falls below the going market rate. Bonds with larger coupons also offer more money to bondholders, both immediately and in the future. Having more money in hand today helps cushion any interest rate blow and allows bondholders to reinvest those funds for a better return later.

The debt instruments that are most susceptible to fluctuations in interest rates are zero-coupon bonds, whose full return is paid at maturity, a time in the future when there is much less certainty about interest rates or economic conditions.

The level of current interest rates can affect how a bond reacts to future changes in interest rates. If interest rates are already high, bonds will be less sensitive to interest rate changes. If interest rates are already low and heading lower, sensitivity increases. For example, if something costs $100 and the price drops by $5, this represents a 5 percent decline in value. But if the same item sells for $50 and there's a $5 decrease, the difference is 10 percent. The same concept applies to interest rates. Both yields and prices of bonds move to a greater degree if interest rates are already low.

Credit ratings are another factor that can come into play. Bonds with better credit ratings can withstand interest-rate volatility better than those with poorer ratings. This is because companies and countries with lower-rated bonds are more likely to suffer financially if interest rates increase. But the upside is that if interest rates fall, lower-rated bonds are likely to do better than higher-rated bonds because they have more potential for improvement.

Inflation Risk

This risk refers to the toll that inflation takes on the purchasing power of the money earned on a bond. If a bond is earning 3 percent a year and inflation is 3 percent, its earnings will be canceled out by higher prices at the supermarket, the gas pump, and so on. The position is even worse, of course, if inflation exceeds interest earnings.

Inflation sends shudders up the spines of bond investors because it causes a bond's coupon rates to decrease in value since the purchasing power of the cash from coupons is less. Unfortunately, although there are some inflation-adjusted bonds available, bonds rarely offer adjustments for inflation. To protect against inflation risk, investors tend to look for a bond interest rate that earns significantly more than the prevailing inflation rate.

Reinvestment Risk

Reinvestment risk is the risk that investors have when they are forced to reinvest the proceeds of one bond maturity at a lower rate than the rate previously earned. If the bond has a callable feature that allows the issuer to redeem the bond prior to maturity, the bondholder will receive the principal payment and now will be holding cash that needs to be reinvested. Of course, the reason why the bond was called was because the issuer can now issue another bond at a lower rate. If market rates are lower, reinvestments will have a detrimental effect on the bond's yield to maturity.

Longer-term bonds are more vulnerable to reinvestment risk because the reinvestment return on coupon payments accounts for a larger percentage of the bond's total return. Shorter-term bonds have fewer coupon payments to reinvest so the reinvestment risk is lower. Of course, unless there are bond terms that require reinvestment, the bondholder can opt to receive the coupon amount and put it into an investment offering a higher return.

Call Risk

As we have discussed, another type of reinvestment risk occurs with callable bonds, such as certain types of corporate bonds, U.S. government-agency bonds, and mortgage-backed securities. A bond issuer is most likely to call a bond when interest rates are falling, since a new bond can be issued at the prevailing lower market rate, thus saving the issuer considerable sums of money in coupon payments. Unless investors are willing accept more risk, they are forced to invest in a new bond at an inferior interest rate.

Default Risk

Any bond investment decision must consider the possibility of default. Sovereign bonds, such as U.S. Treasuries, normally do not default, with some notable exceptions. U.S. Treasuries and bonds of a number of other countries have been considered risk-free and have never defaulted. But there is no guarantee that they will not default in the future. Despite the bad reputation rating agencies received as a result of the subprime crisis in 2008, default rates for investment-grade debt have tended to be low. Nevertheless, history tells us that in the past investors in Argentine bonds, Russian bonds, Chinese bonds were left with worthless paper when those countries defaulted.

In the past, the main area of concern regarding foreign bonds has been focused on emerging market countries, but in 2011 the developed countries of Greece, Ireland, Spain, and Portugal were experiencing strained finances and problems in repaying their debt with the result that their bonds declined dramatically in value and were relegated to junk status in many cases. In the corporate arena there are many high-yielding *junk bonds* issued by companies that have experienced financial distress and have used excess *leverage*. Leverage is normally measured by comparing total debt to cash flow or debt to equity and other indicators of the company's ability to pay.

As a rule, default rates tend to remain low when economic conditions are strong and economies are growing, but rise when conditions become poor and economies are contracting.

Tax Risk

Except for tax-advantaged accounts such as retirement accounts and certain state, local, or country bonds, interest payments from bonds are generally taxable income. This has to be factored into the equation, particularly in times of rising inflation, which can easily lead to net losses.

Event Risk

Catastrophic occurrences, such as a natural disaster, failure to gain regulatory approval for a key product, loss of major markets, or corporate accounting misdeeds (such as the Enron scandal of 2002), can have dire effects on bonds. Leveraged buyouts (where one company uses large amounts of borrowed money to purchase another company) can lead to credit-rating downgrades, as can a leveraged buyout to take a public company private. In both cases, the company may be faced with paying off debt that had not been anticipated by existing bondholders. However, positive events, such as a merger of two strong companies, can improve a bond's credit rating or lead to early retirement of bonds at a premium price.

Event risk can also apply to countries' bonds. A natural disaster destroying infrastructure, a political change, and other such events could lead to a country defaulting on its bonds.

Sector Risk

Bondholders can sometimes suddenly become disaffected by an entire class of bonds in a particular sector of the economy. Sector risk refers to the risk inherent to businesses that produce similar products or services. For example, if the price of oil suddenly rises, sectors dependent on fuel (such as transportation) could see their bonds suffer.

Downgrade Risk

Major credit-rating agencies periodically review a company's financial status and may decide to change its credit rating. If the company's financial situation improves, an upgrade may be warranted. If it has deteriorated, the company may receive a lower rating.

The rating agencies review the company's balance sheet, income statement, cash flow, and other indicators to determine its rating. A great deal of weight is given to whether the firm is able to pay the coupon interest when due and repay the final principal at maturity. Agencies typically flag when a ratings review is imminent by placing the company on a credit watch or review status.

A downgrade (or an upgrade for that matter) can have a marked effect on a bond's attractiveness to investors, particularly if it crosses the investment-grade and non-investment-grade divide. As we saw earlier, a bond that falls beneath this invisible line is called a fallen angel.

As a rule, investors tend to flock to bonds with better ratings and to shy away from downgraded ones. Better ratings can help boost a bond's price, while lower ones can result in price declines as investors wrestle with whether the company can still meet its payment obligations.

A downgrade from a high rating of AAA to AA might not be cause for alarm. A one-time downgrade in a bond's credit rating to a level immediately below its current rating is also not as serious as several downgrades that may occur over the life of the bond. However, a downgrade to a level that puts a bond out of the investment-grade category can be disastrous, since many large pension funds and other organizations are not allowed to buy bonds below investment grade and will thus aggressively sell any bond downgraded below investment grade.

Liquidity Risk

Not every bond on the market is easily tradable. The number of bonds being traded can have an impact on liquidity and on price. Price discounting for highly illiquid bonds may occur in order to tempt buyers. Liquidity is particularly important for bond mutual fund managers who operate open-ended funds where investors may demand an immediate return of their investment. The mutual fund manager must be able to liquidate bonds in his portfolio quickly when such redemption demands take place. Liquidity as such times becomes critical.

Sovereign Risk

Political instability or changes in the government or legislature of a country can have a dramatic impact on investment returns. Not only might this make interest payments questionable, it may even put the repayment of a bond investor's original principal in jeopardy. A military coup, a change in government, a declining economy can all have an impact on a country's ability or willingness to repay its debts and interest payments.

CASE STUDY: DEBT CRISES IN LATIN AMERICA

A regional debt crisis occurred in Latin American in the late 1970s and early 1980s. In their quest for industrialization, several countries (notably Mexico, Brazil, and Argentina) borrowed heavily from international creditors in the 1960s and 1970s when their economies were expanding robustly. By 1983, external Latin American debt had soared to more than US$315 billion, half of

(*continued*)

(*Continued*)

the region's gross domestic product. Interest and principal repayments grew to US$66 billion by 1982, more than five times the figure for 1975.

The global economic recession of the 1970s and 1980s, aggravated by the oil shocks of 1973 when the Organization of Petroleum Exporting Countries (OPEC) quadrupled the price of oil, set the stage for a liquidity crunch. To finance their oil-related deficits, Latin American countries, which had formerly relied on financing from foreign governments and international agencies, began shifting their attention to commercial banks for shorter-term, higher-interest-rate loans. Domestic financial reforms opened the floodgates to a freer flow of capital in and out of a number of countries.

In 1982, Mexico was the first country to declare that it could no longer service its ballooning debt. Other Latin American nations followed soon after, with a major recession the consequence for the entire region and real GDP growth limping along at 2.3 percent between 1980 and 1985.

Argentina experienced another debt crisis during a recessionary period that lasted from 1999 to 2002 and that was accompanied by political and social instability. Warning signs were evident when the country began offering extremely high interest rates—up to 100 percent—on short-term bonds. Even after urgent debt restructuring, the country could only muster payments of 25 cents on the dollar on US$90 billion in outstanding debt. In the wake of the largest sovereign-bond default in history, foreign investment quickly dried up, and the peso depreciated quickly after being allowed to float. The aftermath was crippling inflation.

For failing to honor its obligations, Argentina was branded a financial outcast and denounced by creditors around the world. Although by 2005 its economy and stock market had recovered, the country was still struggling to repay its debt. That year, 76 percent of Argentina's defaulted bonds were swapped for lower-value, longer-term bonds. As of early 2010, the government was trying to settle debts associated with the remaining 24 percent.

Inflation Risk

When a bond is purchased, unless it is a variable rate bond, the rate of return is fixed for the duration of the bond's life. If inflation rears its ugly head, then it is possible that the rate of inflation could rise to a rate higher than the interest rate on the bond. For example, if the bond coupon rate is

5 percent and inflation rises to 8 percent, then the bond holder is obtaining a negative real interest rate. His return on the money he invested is actually declining by 3 percent each year in real terms.

Rating Downgrades

There is always a risk that the major rating agencies such as Standard & Poor's, Moody's, or others will decide to downgrade a bond. If there is a dramatic change in the fortunes of a company or country, so that the possibility of a default rises and the bond is downgraded from a high rating such as AAA to a low rating of B+, the price of the bond would immediately fall, since in many cases institutions who are forbidden to hold non-investment-grade bonds would be forced to sell.

THE YIELD CURVE

While no one can predict the future with certainty, investors in the fixed-income market attempt to decipher what may lie ahead by paying close attention to a graph known as the yield curve, the shape of which telegraphs a host of information about interest rates (both short-term and long-term).

The yield curve plots the interest rates on bonds of different maturities. One yield curve may have interest rates for bonds ranging from 1 year to maturity to 20 years to maturity. Each of those bonds will have a different interest rate yield. Logically, the bonds with the longest maturities would have the higher interest rates. A plot of these yields on a graph will give a line or curve. Of course each day, week, month, and year yield curves change so it becomes a benchmark for investors.

Yield curves have been described as being "normal," "steep," "inverted," "flat," or "humped." In a normal, upward-sloping yield curve, the yields on short-term debt instruments are lower than those on long-term instruments. This is perfectly reasonable, since the longer an investor's money is tied up, the greater should be the expected compensation. A steeper curve with interest on the longest dated bonds substantially higher than the short dated bonds would signal that investors expect interest rates to rise and thus are demanding a higher interest rate for the longer-dated bonds. It could also mean that trust in the company or country issuing the bond is low, and therefore anyone willing to tie up his money in a long-dated bond wants a higher interest rate to compensate for the higher risk. A normal yield curve is a sign of a relatively stable investment environment. In this scenario, rates for one-year bonds are several points below those for 30-year bonds. The psychology underpinning the normal shape is that if investors think the economy will grow and interest rates will rise (in tandem with inflation), they will choose short-term debt instruments to avoid being locked into a long-term investment at today's rates. For the same reason, borrowers would want to issue bonds at today's lower rates (instead of tomorrow's perceived higher rates) for as long a term as possible.

A steep curve occurs when interest rates for the shortest-term bonds are much lower than those for long-term bonds. The drop in short-term rates can be a healthy sign of stronger economic conditions, as it allows banks to borrow at lower short-term rates and then lend at higher long-term rates, creating a nice spread.

An inverted yield curve occurs when short-term rates are higher than long-term rates. Inflation or other factors (too rapid economic growth, for example) that may have led a central bank to tighten credit cause businesses to rush to borrow money in anticipation of conditions becoming worse in the future. If this sentiment carries on too long, the domino effect of the higher cost of short-term borrowing—reducing production, decreasing inventories, and cutting back on labor—can be a harbinger of a coming recession. Of course, an inverted curve by itself is not a foolproof indication of where the economy is heading.

A flat yield curve occurs when short-term and long-term interest rates are virtually the same. This is often seen as a transitional phase between a normal yield curve and an inverted one. Interest rates paid on long-term bonds offer no advantage to investors over short-term ones.

A humped yield curve results when interest rates on short- and long-term bonds are similar, while the rates on medium-term bonds are higher than either short- or long-term bonds. This too is considered transitional, as it is often a stage on the way to an inverted yield curve, although it could also simply be due to a smaller supply of long-term bonds.

There are a number of economic theories surrounding yield curves. Here are some:

Expectations theory: This theory states that long-term interest rates can predict future short-term interest rates. Studies indicate that this hypothesis tends to overstate future short-term rates, probably as a result of the higher risk premium of long-term debt where the yield is more certain.

Liquidity-preference theory: This theory is based on the assumption that longer-term bonds tend to have more market risk and consequently should offer higher yields. The name of the theory derives from the sentiment that investors tend to prefer the liquidity of shorter-term bonds, even if they offer lower interest rates than longer-term bonds. Investors demand a risk premium for committing their money for longer terms and for the increased exposure to default from a longer-term bond.

Market-segmentation theory: According to this theory, market players gravitate to either short-term or long-term investments based on their investment needs. One investor may want to focus on short-term instruments while waiting for the longer-term interest picture to take shape; in contrast, a buy-and-hold strategist might want the security of locking in a certain rate for a number of years.

The yield curve in this scenario reflects the basic market forces of supply and demand for each maturity. Since the majority of investors prefer short-term investments, interest rates for shorter terms tend to be lower than those for longer terms.

SUMMARY

Risk will always be with us, and therefore it must be managed by first recognizing where it is and then assessing possible rewards for certain levels of rick. Thus risk and reward tend to go hand in hand. As a rule, the greater the expected reward, the greater is the risk. All investments carry risk, and it is a mistake to consider any bond as risk-free. There is a wide range of risks found in different types of bonds whether they be government or corporate.

Despite being thought of as conservative investments, bonds are subject to a number of risks. Interest-rate risk is perhaps the greatest worry for investors because of its direct impact on bond prices. Inflation risk refers to the manner in which inflation erodes the purchasing power of money. Reinvestment risk, call risk, default risk, downgrade risk, and liquidity risk are of particular concern to bondholders. Sovereign risk and exchange-rate or currency risk are international factors that investors should also consider, especially in light of major bond defaults in Asia, Russia, and Latin America.

In trying to predict the best times to buy and sell, bond investors pay close attention to the yield curve for indications about where interest rates and economic conditions are heading. The yield curve is an important benchmark that plots the interest rates on a range of bonds, with varying maturities. Typical yield-curve shapes range from normal (upward sloping, with short-term yields paying less than long-term yields) to inverted (short-term rates are higher than long-term ones).

Several economic theories attempt to explain the yield curve and the relationship between yields and maturity. These include the expectations theory, the liquidity-preference theory, and the market-segmentation theory.

QUICK QUIZ

1. What type of risk has the greatest effect on bond prices?
2. What type of bond makes adjustments for inflation?
3. Explain how foreign currency movements can affect the value of coupon payments and principal repayments.
4. What are the main yield curve shapes?
5. What inference can be drawn about a yield curve that is flat?

9
INVESTING METHODS

When considering investment in bonds the first question for investors should be: "Do I want to do this myself, or should I get experts to do it for me." If the inclination is to invest for oneself, the next question should be: "Do I have the time to study bonds intensively?" and "Do I have the inclination to learn more and more about bonds?" If the answer to those questions is "no," then the best way to invest in bonds is through well-managed bond funds of which there are many around the world. A study of available bond funds operated by reputable fund management houses will reveal an abundance of different types of bond funds with an incredible array of choices. In this chapter we will discuss investing in bond funds, but for investors who would like to do it themselves, we will first discuss investing in individual bonds.

INDIVIDUAL BOND INVESTING

Individual bond investing is a challenging task because of the very wide choices available of bonds with varying terms and conditions. The process is, by necessity, complicated and time consuming. Also, building an individual bond portfolio requires a significant amount of capital, since bonds usually sell in denominations of thousands of dollars. Brokers and dealers often require an investment of tens of thousands of dollars to open an account. Normally, an investment of over US$100,000 in a variety of bond types, maturities, and issuers is recommended in order to build a sufficiently diversified portfolio of individual bonds.

One advantage of purchasing individual bonds is that it enables the investor to tailor the portfolio to meet very specific objectives, which could be more than simply ensuring a certain amount of income for a child's education in 10 years. The individual bond investor, for instance, may have certain ethical preferences such as investing only in bonds of environmentally friendly industries. Such specific objectives could be difficult to find in a bond fund. There may also be some unique tax requirements that only a customized portfolio may fulfill. The avid student of interest rates and bond prices can invest in individual bonds in such a way as to meet specific objectives while also maximizing returns.

Of course, investing in bonds actively requires continuous management of interest payments and decisions about how those payments should be invested. Also, monitoring is essential to determine the possibility of rating downgrades, which could affect bond prices. Since some bond prices may not be transparent, investors often have to bargain for the best prices. Liquidity is also of great concern, and the investor may not have the opportunity to sell if no willing buyers are available. In short, individual bond investing requires continuous research and attention.

If you are ready to embark on building you own bond portfolio, then after setting out your general objectives you must establish your investment goals in terms of (1) your time frame, (2) the amount of risk you are willing to tolerate, and (3) your tax status.

TIME FRAME

It is common for investors to have a specific time goal in order to have a certain amount of money sometime in the future. For example, if a parent with a new baby wants to plan for the baby's college education in 20 years it would be prudent to establish a bond portfolio, which after the 20 years would yield the estimated cost of the college tuition. Investors with a house mortgage know when payments are due on the mortgage and can then plan a bond portfolio around those specific future payments.

BOND RISKS

Bond risks can be related to interest rate risk, credit quality risk, call or reinvestment risk, and liquidity risk:

Interest rate risk occurs as a result of interest changes during the life of a bond. For example, when an investor needs to sell his bond before maturity and, in the meantime interest rates have risen, bond prices could have fallen. Selling the bond before maturity in such a case would result in a loss on the original price paid. This risk declines, of course, as the bond maturity dates gets closer.

Credit risk is related to the financial strength of the bond issuer. A bond issuer falling into difficulties could result in that issuer defaulting on bond payments. It is not unusual for a company or country to issue bonds at a time when the financial outlook was good and the bond ratings were high. When company's losses pile up or a country's government has spent too much (so they are unable to meet their interest payment), bond prices fall or even enter into default.

Call or reinvestment risk occurs when a callable bond is redeemed by the issuer prior to maturity when interest rates are falling, thus forcing the bond holder to accept cash and reinvest at a lower interest rate.

NOTE
SAFETY

Someone has said: "The return *of* principal is more important than the return *on* principal." Bond defaults can be disastrous for any portfolio. In the early 2000s, bonds of Lehman Brothers and Washington Mutual were top-rated and considered very safe but suddenly they were junk. This shows that there are not many bonds that can be called ultrasafe, and when they are found, they come at a cost such as very low interest rates. Conditions can change, and change rapidly, so that a bond rated triple A one day could be rated below investment grade in a relatively short period of time.

Liquidity risk occurs when the numbers of buyers and sellers decline so that market turnover shrinks. In such an environment, a bond holder wishing to sell his bonds finds that there are no buyers in the market. This, of course, makes it impossible for the bond holder to sell at a fair price.

Those risks can never be completely eliminated although good research and monitoring can reduce them. However, in addition to researching the financial strength of the bond issuers in which you would like to invest, the best way to reduce risk is to diversify. As a general rule, it's never a good idea to put all your assets and all your risk exposure in a single asset class or investment. You will want to diversify the risks within your bond investments by creating a portfolio of several bonds, each with different characteristics. Choosing bonds from different issuers protects you from the possibility that any one issuer will be unable to meet its obligations to pay interest and principal. Choosing bonds of different types (government, agency, corporate, municipal, mortgage-backed securities, and so on) creates protection from the possibility of losses in any particular market sector. Choosing bonds of different maturities helps you manage interest rate risk.

TAXES

Taxes can have a devastating impact on savers and investors, and any portfolio plan must consider the impact of taxation. For this reason, many investors focus on tax-free bonds offered by governments either at the national, state, provincial, or town level. There is a wide range of possibilities in this regard. For example, some municipal securities offer interest that is exempt from federal income tax and, in some cases, state and local taxes as well.

Because of variables in supply and demand, tax-exempt yields in the municipal market can sometimes be quite attractive when compared to their taxable equivalents.

STRATEGY: PRESERVING PRINCIPAL WHILE EARNING INTEREST

The buy and hold strategy is good for investors who are less interested in obtaining capital gains from the increases in the value of bonds and more interested in wanting to keep their money intact and earning interest. When you invest in a bond and hold it to maturity, you will get interest payments, and receive the face value of the bond at maturity. In a buy and hold strategy, you need not be too concerned about the impact of interest rates on a bond's price or market value. If interest rates rise, and the market value of your bond falls, you should not be concerned, since you will be holding the bond to maturity. Of course, holding on to the bond means you will not be able to invest that principal at the higher market rates.

If the bond you choose is callable, you have taken the risk of having your principal returned to you before maturity. Bonds are typically called or redeemed early by their issuer when interest rates are falling, which means you will be forced to invest the bond principal returned to you at lower prevailing interest rates. For this reason, choosing callable bonds would not be a good policy when using a buy-and-hold strategy

When investing to buy and hold, it is important to focus on the bond interest rate and the credit quality of the issuer. Since you are interested in long-term income, a careful balance should be made. A bond with a lower credit rating might offer a higher yield, but it also carries a greater risk that the issuer will not be able to keep its promises.

LADDERS, BARBELLS, AND BULLETS

Buy-and-hold investors can manage interest rate risk by creating a *ladder portfolio* of bonds with different maturities: for example, 1, 3, 5, and 10 years. A laddered portfolio has principal being returned at defined intervals. When one bond matures, you have the opportunity to reinvest the proceeds at the longer-term end of the ladder if you want to keep it going. If rates are rising, that maturing principal can be invested at higher rates. If they are falling, your portfolio is still earning higher interest on the longer-term holdings you already own. To fund a four-year college education, you could invest in a laddered portfolio of four zero-coupon bonds, each maturing in one of the four consecutive years when the four tuition payments will be due.

With a *barbell strategy*, investments are only made in short-term and long-term bonds, not intermediate term bonds. The long-term holdings should deliver higher interest income than the short-term bonds. However, having some principal maturing in the near term creates the opportunity to invest the money elsewhere if the bond market takes a downturn.

NOTE
ZERO-COUPON BONDS

Zero-coupon bonds are often used to meet future payment requirements, since they can be purchased at a steep discount from the face value, but the face value will then be returned at maturity with interest attributed to the bond during its lifetime, hence the discount. Investors can then invest in zero coupon bonds with maturity dates timed to their specific future needs. The value of zero coupon bonds is more sensitive to changes in interest rates, however, so there is some risk if you need to sell them before their maturity date.

A *bullet strategy* can also be used to yield a specific amount of money at a defined future date. If you are 50 years old and you want to save toward a retirement age of 65, in a bullet strategy you would buy a 15-year bond now, a 10 year bond five years from now, and a five-year bond 10 years from now. Staggering the investments this way may help you benefit from different interest rate cycles, but will result in a bullet payment on your retirement date.

STRATEGY: MAXIMIZING PROFITS

If the goal is to maximize profits, then the focus must be not only on earning higher interest income but on earning capital gains income. Of course, trying to maximize both of those income sources can mean significantly higher risk. Earning higher interest means that you either need to purchase bonds with a longer maturity (since on the normal yield curve, the longer-dated bonds pay higher interest) or purchase bonds issued by organizations that offer a higher bond coupon because they are a higher risk. Longer-maturity bonds are more vulnerable to changes in market value as a result of changes in interest rates. Buying bonds issued by less stable organizations raises the risk profile of your portfolio.

High-yield bonds (sometimes referred to as *junk* bonds) typically offer above-market coupon rates and yields because their issuers have credit ratings that are below investment grade: BB or lower from Standard & Poor's; Ba or lower from Moody's. The lower the credit rating, the greater the risk that the issuer could default on its obligations, or become unable to pay interest or repay principal when due. Of course, the importance of diversification in a corporate bond portfolio is paramount, so as to minimize the possible impact of any single issuer's default. High-yield bond prices are also more vulnerable than other bond prices to economic downturns, when the risk of default is perceived to be higher.

In addition to taking greater risk by purchasing longer maturity bonds and bonds from riskier issuers, an active trading strategy is required to maximize income instead of the buy and hold strategy. This means the investor must consider a whole range of variables impacting his portfolio. High-return investors need to buy a bond when its price is low and sell it when the price has risen, rather than holding the bond to maturity. This means careful

NOTE
BOND SWAPPING

Bond swapping takes place when an investor sells a bond and purchases another one simultaneously. Such swapping can be done for various reasons. One important one is to achieve tax savings. For example, an investor who is holding a bond that has declined in market price since it was purchased can sell that bond at a loss and offset that loss against any taxable capital gains. At the same time, another bond is purchased with the same or similar maturity, price, and coupon to reestablish the position. In the fixed-income arena, swapping is quite appropriate since it is relatively easy to find two bonds with similar features in terms of credit quality, coupon, maturity, and price.

Swapping can also be used to change the quality of the portfolio by swapping one lower quality bond for a higher quality one. It can be used to increase total return by taking advantage of interest rate changes. Swapping to increase quality means that the investor will sell a bond with a lower credit quality rating for one with a higher rating. An opposite swap can also take place, where the investor is willing to take greater risk with the possibility of better returns, by swapping a high quality bond for a lower quality one. At the macroeconomic level an investor may feel that the economy is heading for a recession and therefore wants to swap a lower quality bond for a higher quality one in order to escape any business failure of a particular bond issuer.

Swaps can be used to increase the bond yield by moving from short maturity bonds to longer maturity bonds. Also, to establish better call protection a swap can be used to switch from a callable to a noncallable bond (if there is an expectation that interest rates will fall and issuers will call the bonds that now are paying a higher interest rate than prevailing interest rates).

If the investor's studies show that the general interest level will decline, then a swap may be carried out to move from short-dated bonds to longer maturity bonds. Of course such prognostications regarding interest rates are somewhat speculative and require careful study.

and constant study of interest rates, political events, legal changes, and many other variables impacting bond prices. Bond prices fall when interest rates are rising, usually as the economy accelerates. But those bond prices typically rise when interest rates fall, usually when the central bank is trying to stimulate economic growth after a recession. Within different sectors of the bond market, differences in supply and demand can create short-term trading opportunities.

Various futures, options, and derivatives can also be used to implement different market views or to hedge the risk in different bond investments. Investors should take care to understand the cost and risks of these strategies before committing funds.

BOND TRADING

Bonds are traded over the counter as well as on organized exchanges. There are thousands of securities dealers, including banks and brokerage firms, involved in trading municipal, state, federal, and supranational organization bonds. In the over-the-counter market, operators use phone calls and electronic messaging to buy and sell bonds.

Bond prices in the secondary market are normally quoted in fixed increments such as US$100 based on the par value. Investors can consult a variety of media resources such as newspapers, the Internet, and data services to compare current bond prices. Searches on the Internet can be refined by inputting yields, ratings, prices, and other data. Dealers and banks are, of course, important sources of information.

CHOOSING A BROKER

Bond brokers are financial professionals who deal with institutional or individual investors. The investor can choose from various types of brokers who offer services to meet their needs. A bond broker is needed for most types of bond transactions, although direct purchases such as purchases from the U.S. government for government bonds are possible. The brokerage community is normally divided into three categories: full-service brokers, discount brokers, and online brokers.

Full-service brokers provide a full range of services, including advice, research, custodial, and accounting as well as executing buy and sell orders. They also keep substantial bond inventories on hand as well as purchasing on the market. This means that they can provide liquidity for clients wishing to buy or sell. They can charge a fee or make their money from the difference or spread between the bond that they have in their inventory and the price at which they sell.

Discount brokers execute buy and sell orders, buying from full-service brokers or bond issuers and selling the bonds to investors at a mark-up (commission or fee). They normally would not carry their own bond inventories or provide investment advice to clients.

Online brokers are the newest breed of bond brokers. Operating in both full-service and discount capacities, online brokers tailor their services to the growing ranks of Internet-savvy investors.

Choosing a broker is not a decision that should be made lightly. When evaluating financial professionals, education, experience, credentials, and reputation all have to be taken into account. Are they, for example, registered with the appropriate regulatory authorities? It's important to do background checks offered by various online services and through government organizations as well as industry associations. Investors can also obtain recommendations through their bank, accountant, lawyer, and other financial professionals. It is important to find a broker who has access to and experience in various types of bonds (corporate, municipal, international, and so on).

It is important to learn about prices and fees before investing. Some brokers charge a flat fee, and others receive all or part of the commission or a portion of the dealer's mark-up (the amount the dealer adds to the bond price for his profit when selling) or mark-down (the amount the dealer subtracts from the bond price for his profit when selling) on each bond transaction. In many cases, these fees are not required to be disclosed when an investor buys or sells a bond. However, when an agent, acting on the investor's behalf, charges for services, this fee should be revealed, whether this is in the form of a flat fee, an hourly rate, a commission, or a percentage of the assets the broker manages on the investor's behalf. In any case, it's perfectly acceptable to ask if the agent is willing to negotiate on fees.

BOND FUNDS

Over US$2 trillion is invested in thousands of bond funds all over the world. Bond funds—including mutual funds (open-end and closed-end, actively managed and indexed), exchange-traded funds, and unit investment trusts—offer a convenient and affordable way to invest in a diversified portfolio of bonds, but a bond fund investment can differ from a bond investment in ways that are important to understand.

When you buy a bond fund, you buy shares in a portfolio of bonds that is created or managed to pursue a specific investment objective, such as current income, current tax-exempt income, total return, or to match the performance of a market index. The portfolio might invest in a particular type of bond (government, municipal, mortgage, or high-yield) or a particular maturity range: short-term (3 years or less), intermediate term (3 to 10 years), or long-term (usually 10 years or longer).

Bond fund prices are based on their net asset value (NAV) or the total market value of the portfolio divided by the total number of fund shares outstanding. A fund's NAV changes daily with market conditions and with cash inflows and outflows to and from the fund portfolio.

TYPES OF BOND FUNDS

Bond mutual funds can be actively managed or indexed, open-end and closed-end. *Actively managed bond funds*, as their names suggest, have managers who actively make decisions to buy and sell bonds in pursuit of their investment objective. They sometimes sell bonds at a profit, creating a capital gain, or at a loss if they want to switch to another bond or, in the case of open-end funds, to generate cash to meet redemptions from shareholders.

Passively managed funds or *index bond funds* including *exchange traded funds* (ETFs) are not actively managed but are constructed to match the composition of a given bond index. When the index changes, the portfolio is changed to copy the index holdings.

Sponsors of *open-end bond funds* (unit trusts in the UK) offer new shares and meet the redemption requests of their holders and redeem existing shares continuously, requiring their managers to invest cash coming into the fund and liquidate positions when they need cash to meet redemptions. Investors in open-end funds have the choice to collect their interest income and capital gains or reinvest them automatically in more funds shares.

Closed-end bond funds (investment trusts in the UK) have a fixed number of shares that trade on exchanges similar to stocks at a price that may be above or below net asset value depending on supply and demand. Closed-end bond funds can be indexed or actively managed.

Exchange traded funds (ETFs) represent shares in a basket of bonds that mirrors an index, but the number of shares is not fixed. ETFs trade on an exchange, with shares bought and sold through brokers just like closed-end funds.

Unit investment trusts (UITs) are like closed-end funds in the sense that there are a fixed number of shares. On the trusts' maturity date, the portfolio is liquidated and the proceeds returned to unit holders on a pro rata basis. UITs are usually created by brokerage firms who try to maintain a secondary market for the units but offer no guarantee of liquidity.

Open-end funds accept new investors and allow investors to withdraw their money at any time and to freely buy or sell their shares. *Money-market*

NOTE
ACTIVE VERSUS PASSIVE MANAGEMENT

The debate about whether to invest in actively or passively managed funds will probably rage forever. Active management means that managers are constantly looking for ways to develop a return that beats the market. Some investors take comfort in the thought that people are working hard on their behalf.

Passively managed funds are set up to track the performance of standard market indices and simply invest in the exact bonds representing the index. Some experts advocate investing in both types of funds to obtain the benefits of both—an index fund that consists of a well-diversified portfolio of bonds and a good actively managed fund.

funds are a type of open-end fund or unit trust used by investors to park their money in the short run. They invest in short-term (three months or less), highly liquid securities, which can include U.S. Treasuries, municipal bonds, bank certificates of deposit, and commercial paper. Investors can withdraw their money from these funds at any time. Under normal circumstances, these funds are considered ultrasafe and the chance of losing the value of the original investment is extremely remote. However, during times of crisis with volatile interest-rate fluctuations, the situation can be markedly different.

Closed-end funds are launched at one point in time, investors are accepted at the launch date, and then the fund is closed to further investors so that the number of shares is fixed. Unlike open-end mutual funds, they have a finite number of shares. Since they are closed to any new investors, if an investor wants to liquidate his holdings he must go to the market and sell on the exchange. Just like open-end funds, depending on the fund's objective, the bonds included in these funds may be all of one type, such as corporate bonds, or a combination of various types of bond categories and maturities, such as government, municipal, and so on. Also like open-end funds, they too are actively managed. Closed-end funds are listed and traded on exchanges, like stocks. The price of a share is determined by marketplace supply and demand. This can be higher or lower than the net asset value (NAV), which calculates the price of the fund's underlying fixed-income securities.

EVALUATING BOND FUNDS

When evaluating funds, total costs as well as performance must be examined. It is not wise to buy a fund based on its yield alone. Only those that have had solid returns over several years should be picked. Potential investors should look at the total return, which shows the fund's overall gain or loss over a set period of time. This covers both the income (interest payments) and gains or losses in the price of a bond. Information about bond funds is available in the business press and from research firms such as Morningstar and Lipper Analytical Services. Libraries also subscribe to many of these resources.

BOND INDEX

There are a number of different bond indices used to measure market behavior of different bond categories. Bond investors use these indices to compare the performance of the bond fund they own, or are thinking of buying, against the appropriate index. For example, an investor in an American bond fund might use the Barclays Capital Aggregate (formerly the Lehman Aggregate), the Citigroup BIG, or the Merrill Lynch Domestic Master.

EXCHANGE-TRADED FUNDS

Exchange-traded funds (ETFs) are a special type of mutual fund formulated to track the performance of a specific bond-market index. Bond-market indices are created by financial information services or financial institutions as a means of tracking the bond market or a specific sector of the market, such as government, corporate, or emerging-market bonds, or even a particular maturity or credit-quality bond group. Investors are thus able to gain exposure to a particular market by purchasing such ETFs, which have a number of different brand names.

Like bond-market indices, ETFs are also created and managed by financial firms, but not necessarily by the same institutions that create and manage the index on which they are based. Common brand names for ETFs include iShares, SPDRs (Standard & Poor's Depository Receipts, also known as "Spiders"), Diamonds, and Vipers.

Like closed-end funds they are traded on major stock exchanges, such as the New York Stock Exchange and the American Stock Exchange. This means that investors can initiate trades just as they would with any listed stock. As with listed stocks, price quotes and a trading history for ETFs are available.

The price of a bond ETF is affected by the same factors that influence bond prices: changes in interest rates, in yield spreads (such as the yield difference between a U.S. Treasury bond and other types of bonds), and in the yield curve or the relationship among yields of bonds with different maturities.

While bonds normally pay interest semiannually, ETFs usually distribute dividends monthly. The dividends can include both interest income on the underlying bonds and any capital gains. Since they continuously reinvest any sales proceeds in other bonds, ETFs do not have maturity dates, so that, like closed-end funds, the only way for ETF investors to get their principal back is to sell the ETF shares to someone else in the market.

While open-end mutual funds can be actively managed or *indexed* and where the fund holdings strictly follow the composition of the index, ETFs are always indexed and thus do not require the time and effort involved in running and actively managing a portfolio. Consequently, actively managed open-end funds tend to have higher management fees than passively managed ETFs.

FUND FEES, EXPENSES, AND DIVIDENDS

As with stock mutual funds, fees can vary from fund to fund. There can be a number of fees, including sales fees, management fees, and transfer agency fees. It is therefore important to look at total fees and charges. Investors typically pay an annual fee to the mutual-fund company and may also need to pay a sales charge or *load*. If the fee is paid at purchase, it's called a *front-end load*. A commission paid at sale is referred to as *back-end load*. *No-load funds* do not charge sales commissions, but investors must be aware that such funds have other fees that can be considerable. Dividends from bond funds are normally paid monthly and can be automatically plowed back into the fund if the investor wishes.

LEVERAGING

Some funds are allowed to leverage by borrowing money and using it to increase purchases beyond the capital of the fund. This tactic can generate a better yield when the market is rising, but could also cause investors to suffer losses if the market fails.

FUND VALUATIONS: NET ASSET VALUE

The net asset value (NAV) of a fund is priced at the end of each trading day. The price reflects the total market value of all the securities within the fund, minus expenses, divided by the number of outstanding shares. Because the fund's price fluctuates daily, a return of principal is not guaranteed, and, unlike an individual bond, the fund itself never matures. Also, dividends vary. In the case of closed-end funds or unit trusts, the market price of the fund's shares can vary from the NAV, sometimes selling at a premium to the NAV and sometimes selling at a discount.

NEWS CLIP
RESERVE PRIMARY FUND EXODUS

When it was established in 1970, the Reserve Primary Fund had the distinction of being the United States' first money-market fund. But on September 16, 2008, during Wall Street's financial meltdown, it became only the second mutual fund ever to suffer the stigma of breaking the buck—a reference to the fact that shares in the fund were worth only 97 cents for each $1 (buck) in net asset value. In the money-market fund industry it was considered impossible that such a fund's value would decline below the original $1 per share. It was a standard that was considered virtually inviolate in the money-market fund industry. Up to that time, money-market funds were considered among the safest places to hold cash since they were seen as low-risk, low-return funds that invest in the short-term debt of companies and governments. However, the unthinkable happened because the New York-based Reserve was forced to write down to zero US$785 billion it held in unsecured debt issued by Lehman Brothers Holdings Inc., which filed for bankruptcy protection on September 15, 2008. Panicked investors redeemed US$27.3 billion out of the fund, which until then had had US$62.6 billion in assets.

The action set off a chain reaction of more than US$400 billion in redemptions at other money-market funds. This prompted the U.S. Treasury Department to offer a temporary guarantee program protecting investors who has money-market fund shares as of September 19, 2008. This helped stop the money-market fund outflows.

The first fund to break the buck was the Community Bankers Mutual Fund when each share declined to 96 cents in 1994. Thus each investor lost four cents on each dollar invested and the buck (a dollar) was broken. However, that fund was limited to bankers and did not include retail investors.

SUMMARY

Bond investors can choose from individual bonds, bond funds, exchange-traded funds, or combinations of all three, in accordance with their individual investment goals. Individual bonds are a known quantity—they have fixed yields and maturities, and the principal is returned at a definite point in the future. Individual bonds are also especially useful for those who need income within a certain period of time, such as for a child's college education expenses. But a portfolio of individual bonds requires careful managing and a sizeable financial commitment.

Bond funds provide convenience and diversification. It is considerably easier to buy or sell shares in bond funds than it is individual bonds. However, fund fees and expenses can eat into returns and, unlike individual bonds, the fund's day-to-day value and interest payments are constantly changing. Types of bond funds include money-market funds, mutual funds (open-end and closed-end funds), and unit investment trusts.

QUICK QUIZ

1. What are the main differences between individual bonds and bond funds?
2. What factors should go into the selection of a broker?
3. What is the most common type of bond fund?
4. How does an exchange-traded fund differ from a mutual fund?

10
BUILDING A PORTFOLIO

Creating a bond portfolio not only involves a great deal of research and study but also requires the judgment that comes from experience. It is, of course, necessary to know the fundamentals about different kinds of bonds, the respective merits of individual bonds and bond funds, the workings of the bond market, and the economic factors that could have an impact on values.

CONSTRUCTING A PORTFOLIO

When constructing a fixed-income portfolio, investors should have a clear financial goal in mind. It's a good idea to write down what that mission is (a down payment on a house, paying college tuition, or retirement income, for example) and how it is to be achieved. The written plan should contain details of the investor's attitude toward risk and return, investment strategy (maturities and credit quality), and the techniques to maximize return—such as adding foreign bonds, callable bonds, and swaps (see further on) to the mix.

The next step is deciding whether to pursue a passive or an active management strategy.

Asset Allocation

Asset allocation refers to how investments are distributed among different categories of assets. Asset categories include cash, stocks, bonds, real estate, foreign currency, natural resources, precious metals, and collectables. Many experts regard choosing the correct combination of asset classes as the most important factor in determining a portfolio's returns.

Diversification

Diversification is a strategy of investing in many assets in order to minimize volatility and to ensure more consistent returns (that is, not putting all your eggs in one basket). The key to diversification is investing in instruments that are uncorrelated. For example, a portfolio of safe but lower-yield U.S. Treasuries could be supplemented with higher-yielding but riskier international bonds.

Don't be afraid to diversify by industry, country, issuer, and maturity as well by bond type. This can help smooth out market volatility. When the economy is strong, investment-grade corporate bonds tend to outperform government bonds.

Risk Allocation

A bond portfolio can be classified as conservative (risk-averse), moderate (risk-neutral), or aggressive (risk-tolerant). The degree of risk depends on an investor's age, tolerance for risk, and financial goals. Of course, many investors might choose to stick with ultraconservative instruments, such as money-market accounts, money-market funds, certificates of deposit, and U.S. savings bonds.

Others are willing to explore a variety of risk-return options. For example, a conservative portfolio might focus on government bonds with high ratings; one with a moderate amount of risk could be evenly split among government bonds, high-quality corporate bonds, and convertible bonds and mortgages. An aggressive portfolio might consist of high-grade corporates, emerging markets, mortgage, and high-yielding (junk) bonds.

Rebalancing

Whatever the percentage, a portfolio needs to be as flexible as the bonds themselves.

As we have noted, historically, stocks and bonds have tended to move in opposite directions. When one is up, the other is down. The kinds of bonds that have followed this predictable pattern include government and agency calcbonds, investment-grade corporate bonds, and municipal bonds. When stocks falter, bonds are there to provide both stability and diversification.

Timing

Those who anticipate a fall in interest rates often invest in longer-term bonds in order to profit from the subsequent rise in bond prices. The best time to buy fixed-income investments is when interest rates are high and when the prices of existing bonds with lower interest rates fall. During periods when interest rates are low, investors should bide their time with short-term U.S. Treasury bills or money-market funds until the situation improves.

The five stages of a business cycle are recovery, growth, peak, contraction, and trough (recession). Bonds tend to be better investments at the end of the business cycle than at the beginning when economic activity starts to pick up.

Investors should pay attention to the yield curve. Short-term interest rates are normally lower than long-term interest rates on a normal, upwardly sloping yield curve. A normal yield curve occurs when economic conditions are stable and credit is plentiful.

Investors often attempt to anticipate the direction of interest rates before buying fixed-income investments. If they think interest rates are heading upward, they tend to stick with short-term maturities to avoid being locked into a lower long-term rate. This mass psychology helps produce a normal yield curve. If investors think interest rates are going to fall, they seek out long-term bonds because of their higher rates. This, in turn, leads to an inverted yield curve.

Inflation

While inflation is a major concern for fixed-income investors, this risk can be mitigated by allocating a portion of the investment portfolio to inflation-indexed securities such as government or corporate inflation-protected notes (IPNs) or variable-rate notes (VRNs).

Inflation-protected bonds (such as TIPS in the United States), for example, feature a fixed semiannual coupon, with the principal and interest payout adjusted according to changes in the inflation rate. The corporate version (corporate inflation-protected notes) features a coupon that is adjusted based on changes in inflation and monthly interest payments.

VRNs come in two types—floating-rate notes (FRNs) and step-ups. FRNs have a variable coupon pegged to an interest-rate index such as the U.S. prime rate or LIBOR (London Interbank Offered Rate), plus a spread. The coupon resets every three months.

A step-up bond offers a coupon that increases by a predetermined amount at certain intervals over the course of its term, as outlined in the bond indenture. But these bonds are often callable, which can take some of the luster off their attractiveness.

MANAGEMENT STYLES AND TECHNIQUES

Portfolio management can be styled as passive or active. Passive styles follow a somewhat mechanical and predetermined system, while active styles are more flexible and judgmental.

Passive Management Systems

Buy-and-Hold Strategy With a buy-and-hold strategy, the principal and coupon remain unaffected by changing interest rates because the bond is held to maturity. The idea behind this approach is that bonds are a dependable source of income. In choosing bonds for a buy-and-hold portfolio, investors would examine the quality, terms to maturity, and various other aspects of the indenture, such as callability. It doesn't matter whether the securities are purchased at a premium or a discount because the investor expects to receive the full principal at maturity.

Since selling a bond in hopes of earning a profit is not part of a buy-and-hold strategy, transaction costs are kept to a minimum. The aim is to create a portfolio of high-quality, noncallable instruments (government, investment-grade corporate, municipal bonds) that matches an investor's overall investment goals. The buy-and-hold strategy is particularly useful when interest rates are high and are expected to remain so.

Laddering Technique The laddering technique is one in which a portfolio contains individual bonds of different maturities, the objective being to minimize interest-rate risk and to have cash available on a regular basis to meet future obligations.

Each bond is like a rung on a ladder. Maturities, issuers, credit quality, and yields can all be shuffled to suit the individual's investment goals, and it's a good idea to aim for at least half a dozen maturities—short-term, intermediate, and long-term—to ensure a consistent return plus liquidity. Then, as each bond matures, it can be replaced with a new bond that matches the longest maturity so that the portfolio ladder remains the same.

Some investors design their portfolios so that one or a few bonds mature each year. This way, principal, along with income, is always on hand. As each bond matures, interest can be reinvested along with any unused principal. Many investors who need to save for education expenses ladder their portfolio to pay for annual tuition fees.

The most conservative ladder strategy is investing in short-term Treasury securities. Zero-coupon bonds can be an attractive option, since the bonds are purchased at a deep discount and mature at their face value. Laddering can work equally well with municipal bonds or corporate bonds.

For more yield and where the risk profile permits it, investors might venture into more adventurous territory, such as one or two ratings down from the top AAA investment-grade corporate bonds. Callable bonds should be avoided when laddering, since a call could upset a carefully laid out sequence of maturities.

Barbell Strategy A barbell strategy involves investing in a typically 50:50 split of short-term (2–3 years) and long-term (10 or 20 years) bonds but none of intermediate length. (Here, the portfolio has investment weights on either end but nothing in the middle—much like a barbell.)

The advantage of this strategy is that it offers the anchor of solid interest from longer-term bonds along with a ready supply of cash from short-term maturities, which can either be rolled over into a new round of short-term instruments or moved into longer maturities that have better returns should interest rates rise.

If interest rates fall, the proceeds from short-term bonds can be reinvested elsewhere while long-term bond prices will correspondingly rise, thereby offering the possibility of a capital gain. If interest rates rise, the short-term bonds can be invested at maturity in higher-paying instruments. Longer-term bonds, by their very nature, present more of a risk in a higher interest-rate environment.

Bullet Strategy A bullet strategy is useful for investors who know they will need their principal at a specific point in time and need the *bullet* of bond maturity to hit the *target* time precisely. The strategy is normally executed by purchasing several bonds at different times (to minimize the interest-rate risk), which mature at the same time. For instance, an individual may have to produce a fixed amount of cash for a specific mortgage payment or for college tuition. The goal is to have all of the bonds mature at the same time so the payment can be made.

Indexing Indexing is a semipassive strategy that involves tying the risk-and-return performance of a portfolio to a selected bond-portfolio index, such as the Merrill Lynch Global Bond Index. This differs somewhat from a traditional buy-and-hold strategy because it offers more flexibility and tends to work best with a larger portfolio that can replicate the constituents of a particular bond index. Another perk of index funds is that they cost less in fees than actively managed funds.

Active Management

An active management plan looks for a greater risk-adjusted return than a buy-and-hold strategy. Traders take advantage of interest-rate fluctuations and changes in yield spreads. This, obviously, exposes the investor to greater risk, including a significant loss of principal.

Active traders tend to be high-net-worth individuals or portfolio managers who possess a sophisticated understanding of the bond market. They study interest-rate cycles and apply economic (GDP, inflation, trade balance) and financial (corporate profits, new home sales, retail sales, and so on) data in their quest to improve yields and prices by accurately timing the market. Constant monitoring of the portfolio is required to counter any exposure to market risk.

Four main active management strategies are employed: interest-rate forecasting, valuation analysis, yield spreads, and bond swaps.

Interest-Rate Forecasting Traders try to forecast the direction interest rates will take, when this will occur, and how great the change might be. When rates are rising, they might consider shortening the duration of their portfolios and buying corporate bonds in sectors that stand to gain from consumers' increased willingness to spend on things like vacations and consumer goods.

If the economy turns bearish and rates are falling, bond investors typically benefit. But it's also a time when call risks increase, because issuers see an opportunity to pay lower interest rates on their debt. This is a time to lock in longer-term bonds with higher coupon rates and to look more closely at bonds in sectors like banks, consumer staples, and utilities, which are less influenced by economic ups and downs.

Valuation Analysis This strategy focuses on buying undervalued securities and selling overvalued ones. Just as with stocks, bonds can trade at less than their intrinsic value. Traders calculate the market-based return it takes for a bond to be a worthwhile investment (that is, its required yield) and discount the future cash flows in order to make a useful comparison. They can then exploit any price discrepancies in bonds that may appear quite similar in terms of credit ratings, maturities, issuer, and liquidity, thus turning a tidy profit.

Yield Spreads The yield spread is the difference between the yields on any two debt instruments. For example, if one bond pays 5 percent and another pays 4 percent, the yield spread is 5 percent − 4 percent = 1 percent. A number of factors, including the instrument's maturity, credit rating, coupon payment, sector, or issuer, can affect the yield spread.

Investors can profit by accurately predicting changes in yield spreads. The typical flight-to-safety reaction of investors during economic downturns can cause yield spreads to widen. When this happens, potential gains may await the investor who stakes out careful positions in riskier securities, where the yield spread is greatest.

Since transaction fees can eat into the gains from active trading, it behooves investors to make sure that the yield spread is wide enough to still make a profit.

Bond Swaps A bond swap is, as its name implies, the sale of one bond and the simultaneous purchase of another, often for the same price. Investors engage in bond swaps in an effort to improve their overall portfolio performance. This may involve swapping a bond with a lower coupon for a higher one, creating tax losses, or changing the portfolio's maturity structure or credit characteristics.

Since longer-term bonds pay a higher rate of interest than shorter-term instruments, lengthening maturities can boost yields. One caveat is that the prices of longer-term bonds are more sensitive to interest-rate changes. It may also make sense to swap a bond with a higher credit rating for a bond with a lower rating if the yield between the two has widened, but this should be done with caution.

Probably the most common reason behind bond swaps is that they allow investors to improve their tax position. The aim is to sell a bond that is worth less than its original purchase price in order to claim the loss against tax that year and replace it with a similar bond whose gains will not be taxable as income until maturity. This way, losses on the first bond can be used to offset the taxable gains from the second bond later on.

Passive management investors would do well to familiarize themselves with active management strategies, even if they do not plan to employ them. This particularly applies to investors who may have holdings in actively managed bond funds.

NOTE
AVOIDING MISTAKES

- Don't let a high yield get in the way of common sense. The old saying applies: "If something sounds too good to be true, it probably is." Always evaluate what the risk factors are.
- Look for bond funds that charge reasonable management fees. Remember, there is no free lunch in the investment world. A higher fee may come with much better service and performance.
- Check the performance of a bond fund over a period of at least five years and compare it with similar funds.
- Before buying a bond, be sure to read the prospectus. Don't buy on tips or hunches.
- A buy-and-hold strategy is better than trading too often because fees will eat into profits.
- Don't invest in securities that you do not understand or that are too complicated. There are many other alternatives.

INDIVIDUAL REQUIREMENTS

The percentage of a portfolio that should be invested in fixed-income instruments should be determined by the investor's age, income, comfort level, and financial goals. Generally, the older the investor, the greater the percentage that should be invested in bonds. A steady income from interest payments at retirement is often more comforting to retirees than gauging the unpredictable returns of stocks. Once the bond weighting of a portfolio is decided, then the type of bonds selected in the bond portfolio will depend on the risk appetite and requirements of the investor.

Portfolio Composition and Age

Younger investors are likely to be more risk-tolerant and able to invest in lower-rated bonds with higher yields. Non-investment-grade bonds would not be suitable for older investors with a shorter timeframe and a need for steady and secure income, even if the yields may not be as high as low-rated bonds. For the adventurous investor, there is always the possibility that the credit rating or company fundamentals on these securities will improve.

Investors will likely have different financial needs and goals throughout their lives. Younger investors may have marriage, a new home, or paying off college loans on their minds. An expanding family, a larger home, or saving for their children's college costs may be goals for those in their middle years. Later in life, being able to retire comfortably may be a prime objective.

Irrespective of age, bonds should be part of every investor's investment plan. Following are suggestions regarding the role that bonds might play in a portfolio at different stages of life.

Young Investors With an investment horizon that stretches several decades into the future and a likely higher tolerance for risk (losses at this stage can be made up in later years), maximizing capital should be the young investor's main goal. This might entail considering higher-yielding, higher-risk instruments—including, perhaps, high-yield bonds, emerging-market bonds, and other exotic fare—because of their potential for greater returns. Although they are more volatile, international bonds can also function in a hedging capacity.

Even though there's plenty of time for recovery in the event of a loss, it's prudent to balance an aggressive stock portfolio with lower- and medium-risk bonds since stocks and bonds tend to move in different directions. If money is tight, a balanced fund of stocks and bonds is a good starting point.

This is also the stage in which to start cultivating good financial habits, such as investing on a regular basis (see Note, following) to help ensure a comfortable retirement.

Learn to juggle present obligations—bills, mortgage payments, a new car, or a wedding—with future needs. For example, if you plan on buying a house in five years, consider investing in low-risk U.S. Treasuries or highly rated investment-grade corporate bonds that are timed to mature when the money is most needed.

NOTE
GOOD HABITS

Dollar-cost averaging is an excellent financial strategy for building financial discipline and enhancing a portfolio. It means investing a fixed amount of money at periodic intervals (usually each month) in mutual funds, in this case bond funds. The aim is to spread the amount invested over a period of time in order to reduce the risk of losing value in a market downturn shortly after making a large single investment. This strategy lowers the average cost per share over time.

Research is essential, whether that means researching each bond or bond fund yourself or consulting a reputable financial advisor.

Middle-Aged Investors With their income probably higher now than it was when they were younger, these are crucial years for investing and accumulating a nest egg. This is also when planning for retirement and saving for their children's education should come into play. Capital growth should still be the primary goal, but because of the shorter investment horizon it may be wise to rebalance the portfolio with an eye toward decreasing risk. This strategy offers a degree of protection against significant or prolonged stock market declines.

Diversification should be an important part of the financial strategy at this stage, and bonds should play an increasingly important role because they provide steadier returns and are a more reliable stream of income than stocks. Investors who are willing to trade a bit more risk for possibly higher returns might allocate a portion of their funds to higher-yield or longer-term bonds.

To meet major financial goals, such as college tuition or retirement, the investor might consider buying zero-coupon bonds that will mature in the years when they are most needed. Sold at a deep discount from their face value, these bonds should be kept in a tax-deferred account since the interest on zero coupons is taxable, even though it cannot be spent until the bond matures.

Older Investors Protecting capital should be the driving force behind any financial strategy as retirement looms. Shifting from stocks to bonds will decrease the potential for losses and the uncertainties associated with stock-market volatility. Many advisors suggest that bond holdings should be increased to 50 percent or more of the portfolio at this stage. Where possible, risk can be reduced by investing in different issuers, market sectors, maturities, and credit qualities, although this can add up to a significant cash outlay.

Individual bonds offer the promise that the principal outlay will be returned upon maturity while bond funds do not. However, bond funds, unit trusts, and exchange-traded funds hold out the prospect of greater diversification and a much lower minimum cash layout than individual bonds.

At least until 2011, when they were downgraded by some rating agencies, U.S. Treasuries have been considered the most conservative and safe investments. They still stand high on the list of safe investments and, for U.S. citizens, have the advantage of being exempt from state and local income taxes. Throughout the world, government bonds or municipal bonds often have various tax advantages, so that those advantages, combined with the relative safety of such bonds, should make them an important part of a older person's portfolio.

Longer life expectancies are creating a pressing need for longer-term financial planning. During the Depression years, overall life expectancy in the United States was 59. Today, it's 75 for men and 81 for women. While added longevity is the gratifying result of improved medical treatment and nutrition, people's savings are being stretched to pay for those added years.

Some financial experts say that it takes at least 70 percent of preretirement income to adequately maintain a person's current lifestyle after retirement. Some have suggested the figure is closer to 90 percent. A good rule of thumb to go by when deciding how much you can safely spend each year should be based on your life expectancy. An easy way of calculating how much of a nest egg you'll need when you retire is to figure out how much it will cost you to live per year at age 65 and multiply by 20, when you will be in your mid-80s.

However, although the quest to preserve capital is of paramount importance at this stage, it would be a mistake to have a portfolio consisting entirely of bonds. Historically, stocks have been a better bet for staying ahead of inflation, and they also provide much-needed diversification. The long-term return on stocks has been about twice that of bonds over the past 80 years or so.

Many of today's retirees are living longer, more active lives. Long-term bonds may seem tempting because of their higher yields, but they should be approached with caution since the principal can be at risk if market conditions change drastically or the bond is sold before maturity.

Inflation can seriously erode spending power for those living on a fixed income; therefore an option is to consider investing in government bonds that pay a fixed coupon rate but whose principal is adjusted to keep pace with increases in inflation.

THE MAGIC OF COMPOUNDING

Compounding is the astonishing power that time can have on your investments. It refers to the process of earning interest on interest. The longer the time horizon, the more compounding can work its magic.

NOTE
THE RULE OF 72

A useful calculation for bond investors who want to know how long it will take for each bond in their portfolio to double in value is the Rule of 72. Here, the number 72 is divided by the yield-to-maturity (YTM) of each bond to get the target date. For example, it would take 18 years for a bond paying a 4 percent YTM to double in value ($72/4 = 18$). If you want to double your money in, say, 16 years but don't know what yield would be required, use basic algebra: $72/x = 16$. $x = 4.5$ percent. This rule is not completely accurate, however, since it assumes that all interest is reinvested at the same rate every year.

For example, $1,000 invested at 5 percent would return $1,050 after one year. The $50 gain is simple interest, or the interest earned on the original principal. After 10 years, the simple interest would total $500 ($1,000 × 10 × 0.05 percent = $1,500). But if $1,000 had been invested at 5 percent for 10 years and the interest compounded, the total amount would be $628.89. The additional $128.89 is the interest earned on interest.

The difference widens over time. The simple interest on a $10,000 bond paying an annual coupon of 5 percent over 40 years would be $20,000, but if all of the coupon payments were reinvested at the same interest rate, the total would amount to $70,399.88.

SUMMARY

For disciplined investors who seek a steady appreciation of their assets, bonds are an ideal choice at every stage of life. They can function as the basic building block of a diversified portfolio, providing a regular stream of income, and serving as a hedge against stock-market volatility. Asset allocation (overall portfolio mix) and diversification are two key concepts in successful investing. Both are important in reducing an investor's vulnerability to changes in any single economic determinant, such as interest rates.

The percent of bonds in a portfolio will depend on an individual's age, income, financial goals, and comfort level. As a general rule, the best time to buy fixed-income securities is when interest rates are high and when the prices of bonds with lower interest rates fall. It's important to have a clear financial goal in mind when building a portfolio and in helping to determine whether to pursue an active or passive management strategy.

QUICK QUIZ

1. Explain why asset allocation and diversification are two important concepts for successful investing.
2. When is the best time to buy fixed-income instruments?
3. Explain the different strategies used in active and passive management.
4. How would your investment strategy change at different stages of life?
5. What is a bond swap, and what is its purpose?

11

Q&A ON BOND INVESTING

Following is a list of common questions about bond investing. The answers are intended to offer bond investors guidance on key topics.

At the end of this chapter, following the Quick Quiz Answers, is a list of useful websites that offer additional information about bonds and investing, accompanied by a glossary of common bond terms.

WHAT ARE SOME COMMON MISTAKES THAT BOND INVESTORS MAKE?

Lack of diversification. Diversification offers a degree of protection: If one bond investment sours, then your chances of investment survival are better. This is difficult for the small investor because a bond portfolio needs to be sizable in order to obtain a variety of bonds and minimize trading and administrative fees. Many bonds sell in denominations of thousands of dollars, and dealers may require an investment of tens of thousands of dollars to open an account.

Also, using yield as the sole basis for buying is a mistake. A high-yielding bond is tempting during periods when interest rates are low and the stock market is performing poorly. In the search for better returns, it is tempting to go for bonds paying higher yields. However, this implies that the investor will be taking higher risks because the riskier bonds will offer higher yields: the higher the yield, the greater the risk. A wiser course is to make a decision based on a number of factors including your tolerance for risk, the bond's credit rating (based not only on a bond rating agency but the investor's own research regarding the credit reputation and strength of the issuer), and the bond's prospective liquidity.

IS IT BETTER TO BUY A BOND AT A DISCOUNT THAN AT A PREMIUM?

Investors are willing to pay a premium for a bond either because it has a higher safety rating or because it comes with a higher interest rate. Discount bonds sell for less because their coupon is typically lower or they have a lower safety rating. Assuming the credit rating is equal when deciding which to buy, what really matters is the yield to maturity. This allows you to make an accurate comparison between the value of bonds that have different coupon rates and maturities.

WHAT ARE THE SAFEST BONDS IN WHICH TO INVEST?

Up to recent times U.S. Treasuries or bonds issued by financially stable governments were considered the safest from a default perspective. However, news in 2011 about bond default in the eurozone and also questions regarding the viability of U.S. Treasuries have challenged the assumption of the safety of government bonds. History is littered with government bond defaults, however; in the context of all bonds issues globally such defaults are relatively rare. While governments do not normally default, all bonds, even U.S. Treasuries, are subject to market risk from fluctuating interest rates. Shorter-term maturities usually have less market risk than longer-term bonds.

Inflation protection bonds where the principal is automatically adjusted to keep pace with some price index, gives investors protection from inflation. Even though the coupon rate remains the same, the interest payments increase because they are based on the inflation-adjusted principal. At maturity, the investor receives the original face value plus all of the added inflation adjustments. Of course, the impact of taxes must always be considered, and each country and issuing area will have their own, and often significantly different taxes, that would impact a bond buyer, depending on the nationality of both the buyer and issuer.

WHAT HAPPENS TO A CORPORATE BOND IF THE CORPORATION GOES BANKRUPT?

Each country's laws regarding bankruptcy are different and must be examined. The good news is that normally bond holders take precedence over stock holders. So in the case of bankruptcy and liquidation of the company's assets, the bond holders would normally be paid before the holders of shares in the company. The recovery process can be expensive and take a long time, but there are many cases where the bond holders eventually obtained a significant portion of their investment but certainly not all.

WHAT IS A GOOD TIME TO BUY BONDS?

The best time to invest is when you have money. High-quality bonds that are bought and held to maturity will provide a dependable stream of income and the return of your principal, regardless of what happens to interest rates. Check the coupon rate and see if the interest they pay justifies your investment and matches your tolerance for risk. But for those planning on trading their bonds before maturity, interest-rate changes can lead to a capital gain or loss. Most personal financial advisors recommend that bonds account for a portion of a diversified individual investment portfolio, along with stocks and cash.

WHY WOULD I SELL MY BOND BEFORE MATURITY?

Different reasons can be behind an investor's decision to sell a bond before it matures. Although a buy-and-hold strategy is considered the best long-term approach, there are times when it makes sense to sell.

For example, a change in financial circumstances may make it necessary for an investor to gain access to principal. Others may see an opportunity for a capital gain if interest rates fall and the bond has appreciated enough in value to make selling worthwhile. Some investors may also want to offset taxable gains in one investment with a loss in another, which is where bond swapping comes in.

WHAT SHOULD I DO IF THE CREDIT RATING ON MY BOND CHANGES?

When a bond is assigned a lower credit rating, the price usually goes down. When the credit rating is upgraded, the price could go up. In the event of a change in the credit rating, an investor should re-evaluate whether to keep the bond or not, and whether it still fits in with one's investment objectives. A credit rating downgrade could be a default warning, and therefore such rating changes should be taken seriously. A careful study of the reasons for the downgrade is essential.

WHAT ECONOMIC SIGNS SHOULD I PAY ATTENTION TO?

Keep an eye on economic growth and inflation. The GDP growth of a nation and consumer and wholesale prices will have an impact on interest rates and thus bond prices. But those two factors are not the only variables to watch. Government policies have a critical impact. What is the central bank of a country doing? What are their policies and plans? How about the government budget? Are they planning to spend more or less? Will they be borrowing more in order to meet budget requirements? Also, what is happening in the country's banking system? Are banks flush with cash but having difficulty in finding borrowers? How about retail sales, the unemployment rate, corporate profits, corporate balance sheets, the consumer confidence index, new home sales, and other related factors? All these should be studied to ascertain the direction of interest rates.

CAN CREDIT AGENCY RATINGS BE TRUSTED?

Rating agencies have been criticized in recent years over conflicts of interest because they earn revenue from the bond-issuing organizations they rate. Others claim that the agencies are too slow to lower the ratings of companies that are in trouble. Despite these weaknesses, credit ratings are still relied upon heavily by most individual investors and by many other market participants, including the issuers themselves. This is because they provide an historical snapshot of a company's ability to service its debt obligations and to continue to do so in the future. They can also be an important indicator of the current financial health of a company.

Credit ratings are one tool (albeit not a perfect one) that should be evaluated in deciding whether or not to buy a company's bonds. Investors should also consider other factors, such as a bond's call and put provisions, the expenses and fees associated with buying a bond, and the investor's investment goals and objectives.

WHAT IS THE RELATIONSHIP BETWEEN THE STOCK AND BOND MARKETS?

The relationship between stocks and bonds is a complex one. Many have noticed that often their prices move in opposite directions. When the stock market is bullish, money tends to pour into stocks and not bonds. When the economy stumbles, stock prices fall, and investors seek out the perceived safer haven of bonds. However, that relationship does not hold in all situations, and the complexity of the market will often surprise. Nevertheless, it can be said that generally bond prices will move inversely to interest rates. If interest rates rise, bond prices fall: when interest rates fall, bond prices rise.

WHAT SHOULD I DO WITH MY COUPON PAYMENTS?

If you don't have immediate need for the money, it is best to reinvest all of your coupon payments to gain the maximum amount from the power of compounding. This helps minimize the impact of inflation on your bond holdings. Some advisors recommend opening a dedicated account so that the payments will automatically be reinvested. The key is to avoid letting them languish in low-yielding accounts. If you have invested in a bond fund, however, you can direct that your interest payments be plowed back into the fund.

WHAT ARE BOND INTEREST RATES BASED ON?

Many bond interest rates are pegged to specific government bonds, such as U.S. Treasuries. A benchmark is the minimum interest rate, plus a premium, that investors will demand to invest in a non-Treasury security with a similar maturity. A benchmark rate is associated with a safe, conservative investment, since higher interest rates carry more risk. Of course, from an overall perspective, interest rates on bonds and other fixed-income investments must respond to changes in inflation rates. The higher the inflation rate, the higher the interest rates.

SUPPOSE I INVEST IN BONDS AT THE WRONG TIME AND INTEREST RATES GO UP—WHAT CAN I DO?

The price of your bonds will decline, but you may be able to benefit in the long run. Higher interest rates mean that you can invest your semiannual coupon payments in a bond with the higher prevailing rates. Waiting for interest rates to rise before you buy is not the best strategy. That's like trying to guess when stock prices will be at their lowest.

If the thought of rising interest rates—and thus lower bond prices—sends chills up your spine, buy shorter-term bonds (probably no more than five years) to limit price volatility. The drawback of this, however, is generally the lower interest rates that short-term bonds pay.

QUICK QUIZ ANSWERS

CHAPTER 1

1. Bonds offer a steady income and return on investors' money. Although their prices can be volatile, investors who buy and hold to maturity will receive a regular income stream and return of principal (at maturity) on which they can depend. Bonds have been used to raise money to pay for infrastructure such as new roads, schools, factories, corporate acquisitions, and other investments. Over the years, many major projects have been financed by bond issues. Government bonds enable governments to meet their expenditure needs while corporate bonds enable companies to make their necessary capital investments.
2. Government and corporations choose to issue bonds since raising money through such means can often be done to provide for payment over a longer term than bank financing and, if the credit rating of the issuer is good, can be done at lower interest rates than bank rates. There are often certain tax benefits for the investor enabling the issuer to obtain a lower interest rate. Companies sometimes prefer to issue bonds instead of shares since share issues would result in dilution of existing shareholders' equity.
3. Bonds would be more appropriate for investors who are not looking for spectacular growth and are content with earning a steady income and knowing that the principal investment will be returned at a future data.
4. There is no single strategy that is the best; the appropriate strategy will depend on the investor's personal needs and financial resources.

CHAPTER 2

1. The bond market operates as an over-the-counter entity because of the large variety of bond issues with different characteristics. The liquidity of many of the bond issues can be small, thus requiring a specialized and over-the-counter market.

2. The three categories are issuers (organizations that are looking to borrow money), investors (individuals or institutions that provide capital) and intermediaries (market players such as brokers and bankers that bring issuers and investors together).
3. Steps include: Finding an underwriter; Invitation by the lead manager to potential comanagers to underwrite the bond; Production of a prospectus or offering document; Inclusion of an audit report prepared by auditors in the offering document; A selling group agreement between lead manager and others in the syndicate; Establishment of a gray or unofficial market before bond officially announced; Newspaper notice (tombstone) to publicize bond issue.
4. Economic factors that can affect bond values include: changes in interest rates, since a move by central banks to raise interest rates would cause bond prices to fall; currency movements, where a stronger currency can increase the attractiveness and price of the bonds issued in that currency; and inflation, which affects the real return of the bond and hence the price.
5. TRACE is the Transaction Report and Compliance Engine system, which allows public dissemination of real-time transaction and price data on U.S. bond trading the secondary market. It improves transparency by allowing users to confirm that they are paying a fair market price for their bonds as well as the markup brokers are charging.

CHAPTER 3

1. Investment-grade bonds are bonds with a credit rating that is considered to be safer and less likely to default than non–investment-grade bonds, which have a sub-investment grade, and thus are more speculative and sometimes referred to as *junk bonds.*
2. Major users of credit ratings are investors, market participants, and regulators. Ratings are very important to investors who do not have the time and resources to investigate the background and viability of the bond issuer.
3. The Nationally Recognized Statistical Rating Organization (NRSRO) is a nationally recognized status granted by the U.S. Securities and Exchange Commission (SEC) to ten ratings agencies. The ratings issued by these recognized agencies are considered credible measures of creditworthiness for regulatory purposes.
4. Credit ratings evaluate an organization's ability to meet its obligations.
5. The two controversies are: first, conflicts of interest, because the rating agencies earn their revenues from the companies they rate; and, second, for failing to lower their ratings quickly enough when a company is in trouble.
6. An investment-grade bond which has been downgraded to non–investment grade.

CHAPTER 4

1. The four types of U.S. Treasuries are:
   - Treasury Bills, which are short-term government securities with maturities ranging from a few days to 52 weeks.
   - Treasure Notes, which are government securities with maturities of 2, 3, 5, 7 and 10 years.
   - Treasury Bonds, which are long-term debt obligations with a maturity of 30 years.
   - Treasury Inflation-Protected Securities, which are securities whose principal is adjusted by changes in the Consumer Price Index.

2. Only governments can issue risk-free securities because they have the full backing of the country's economy and can issue more currency to pay the bond.
3. UK gilts are issued in pounds sterling by the UK government, while U.S. Treasuries are issued in U.S. dollars by the U.S. government.
4. TIPS were created to retain value against inflation.
5. Agency bonds are bonds issued by various government agencies while municipal bonds are issued by local municipalities. Agency bonds are structured to meet several different needs of the government agency while municipal bonds tend to raise money for ongoing expenditures or capital investments such as roads, airports, and so forth.

CHAPTER 5

1. Companies issue corporate bonds to raise debt finance instead of issuing shares or obtaining a bank loan.
2. Secured bonds are backed by collateral such as real estate or other assets, while unsecured bonds have no collateral guarantee and are only backed by the issuer's name or credit standing.
3. Convertible bonds allow investors to convert the bond into equity at some point in the future.
4. Junk bonds are high-yielding bonds rated below investment-grade status by major rating agencies; therefore, they may have a higher risk of default.
5. Mortgage-backed securities are bonds backed by a pool of mortgages.
6. The subprime mortgage crisis was caused by the issuing of mortgages to home buyers unable to meet the mortgage payments as a result of the mortgage amount being too large or the house prices falling so that rental yields were too small to meet the mortgage payments. As a result there was a rise in housing foreclosures. Most importantly, the low rated mortgages were securitized and bundled into Collateralized Debt Obligations (CDOs) and sold to investors who were not aware of the low quality of the mortgages. In addition Credit Default Swaps, a type of insurance policy, insuring the CDOs against default, were issued in

massive amounts. When the CDOs collapsed the CDS issuers such as AIG, the world's largest insurance company, found that they were unable to make good on the policies that they issued and thus faced bankruptcy.

CHAPTER 6

1. In March 1989, during a financial crisis in Latin America, Brady bonds, named after U.S. Treasury Secretary Nicholas Brady, were created in order to convert bank loans to primarily Latin American countries into a variety of new bonds after many of those countries defaulted on their debt. The key to success of the Brady Bonds was the fact that commercial banks were able to exchange their claims on Latin American countries into instruments that could more easily be traded thus allowing them to get the debt off their balance sheets.
2. Yes, defaults of bonds issued by governments can occur. Most defaults by government are the result of policies that favor a default on foreign debt rather than an increase in taxes or a reduction in government spending—in other words, political expediency. The so-called debt trap results when a debtor finds that the payments due on a loan are higher than income, and they are forced to borrow more to pay off existing debt.
3. Eurobonds are bonds issued in a currency other than the country or market in which the bonds originate. They are favored because these bonds fall outside the regulatory jurisdiction of a single country and thus allow for greater flexibility.
4. The TED spread indicates the difference in interest rates between three-month U.S. Treasuries and the three-month LIBOR. This spread can be used as a credit-risk indicator since U.S. T-bills are considered risk-free, while the LIBOR rate reflects the credit risk of lending to commercial banks.
5. Currency swaps are an agreement between two parties to exchange the principal, interest payments, or both, of a bond or loan in one currency for another currency. They are used in cases where the investor may not want take the risk of holding a particular currency.
6. Interest rate swaps are normally used to exchange fixed-interest payments or variable-rate interest payments. For example, an investor or borrower who expects interest rates to rise will want to swap his variable rate loan for a fixed interest loan. On the other side, a borrower who expects interest rates to fall would be will to swap his fixed interest loan into a variable rate loan.

CHAPTER 7

1. All bonds have a bid price and an ask price. The bid price is the price offer made by a bond buyer. In a table of bond prices, the bid price is normally shown on the left side column. The ask price, or the price offered by bond sellers, is normally shown on the right.

2. When a coupon-paying bond is purchased, accrued interest is incorporated into the price. For zero-coupon bonds, they are priced at a discount from their principal value to make up for the interest not paid.
3. The coupon income increases the bond's total return.

CHAPTER 8

1. Changes in interest rates as well as the chances of default have the greatest effect on bond prices.
2. Inflation-linked bond such as the Treasury Inflation-Protected Securities (TIPS) makes adjustments for inflation.
3. If the currency in which the bond was denominated strengthened against the investors' home currency, then the value of the coupon payments and principal repayment would normally increase by the same percentage. The reverse is also true.
4. Yield curves are commonly described as being normal, steep, inverted, flat, or humped.
5. A flat yield curve occurs when short-term and long-term interest rates are virtually the same.

CHAPTER 9

1. When you buy an individual bond, you are buying the debt of one government, organization, or company. When you buy a bond fund, you buy shares in a portfolio of bonds that is created or managed to pursue a specific investment objective. Since the fund is more diversified the chances of loss is lower.
2. Factors such as education, experience, credentials, and reputation all have to be taken into account when selecting a broker.
3. Common types of bond funds include money-market funds, mutual funds (open-end and closed-end funds), and unit investment trusts.
4. Exchange-traded funds (ETFs) are a special type of mutual fund formulated to track the performance of a specific bond-market index, while mutual funds allow the investor to buy shares in a portfolio of bonds, which is created or managed to pursue a specific investment objective, such as current income, current tax-exempt income, total return, or to match the performance of a market index.

CHAPTER 10

1. They are important because they help reduce an investor's vulnerability to changes in any single economic determinant.
2. Generally, the best time to buy fixed-income securities is when interest rates are high and when the prices of bonds with lower interest rates fall.
3. Passive styles follow a more mechanical and predetermined system, while active styles are more flexible and judgmental. Examples of

passive management styles include the buy-and-hold strategy, laddering technique, barbell strategy, bullet strategy, and indexing. Active management strategies include using such techniques as interest-rate forecasting, valuation analysis, yield spreads, and bond swaps.

4. Generally, the older the investor, the greater the percentage that should be invested in bonds. Younger investors are likely to be more risk-tolerant and able to invest in equity and lower-rated bonds with higher yields. For older investors, protecting capital would be the driving force behind any financial strategy as retirement looms.
5. A bond swap is the sale of one bond and the simultaneous purchase of another, often for the same price. Investors engage in bond swaps in an effort to improve their overall portfolio performance.

USEFUL WEBSITES

www.about.com An online neighborhood of helpful experts who share their knowledge about a variety of subjects, including bonds.

www.investinginbonds.com A primer on the ABCs of bonds from the Securities Industry and Financial Markets Association (SIFMA).

www.municipalbonds.com An overview about municipal bonds, what's for sale, how to buy, and details on the latest trades.

www.bondbuyer.com After perusing www.muncipalbonds.com, you can read all about municipals in this daily newspaper devoted to municipal bonds.

http://finance.yahoo.bonds Sections on investing, news and opinion, personal finance, and building a bond portfolio, in addition to the latest rates on U.S. Treasury bonds, municipal bonds, and corporate bonds.

www.morningstar.com Provides information about bond funds and about fixed-income and high-yield bonds for individual investors.

www.bondsonline.com Offers a comprehensive array of information, news, quotes, and more.

www.aaii.com The American Association of Individual Investors (AAII) has information and research to help individual investors effectively manage their assets.

www.ici.org The Investment Company Institute is the national association of the U.S. investment company industry. Statistics, FAQs, and investor education resources can be found on its website.

www.smartmoney.com Articles and columns about bonds and other aspects of investing.

www.kiplinger.com Type in "bonds" in the search engine, and hundreds of archived articles about bonds are at your fingertips.

www.fool.com The Motley Fool website offers news, analysis, and commentary that provide a wide range of financial solutions for all types of investors.

www.bloomberg.com Nuts-and-bolts financial data on interest rates for government bonds, corporate bonds, and key rates.

http://money.cnn.com Bond charts articles and interest rates in one comprehensive package.

http://apps.finra.org The Financial Industry Regulatory Authority's website offers an educational section on bond investing.

GLOSSARY

This Glossary is a list of key terms you may have come across in the reading of this book. New terms and definitions are constantly being created so no list can be comprehensive.

Accreted Value
The current value of a zero-coupon municipal bond, taking into consideration the amount of interest earned and automatically reinvested.

Accrued Interest
(1) The amount of interest accrued on an issue, from its date to the date of delivery to the original purchaser. The purchaser usually pays this to the issuer as part of the purchase price. (2) Interest that has been earned but not yet paid.

Adjustable-Rate Mortgage (ARM)
A mortgage loan with an interest rate that may change at regular intervals. Changes in the Treasury bill rate or the prime rate can affect the rate.

Amortization
Gradually eliminating a liability by making regular payments over a period of time.

Arbitrage
An investment strategy that attempts to profit by taking advantage of price differentials between different markets.

Ascending, or Positive, Yield Curve
The interest rate structure that exists when long-term interest rates exceed short-term interest rates.

Ask Price
Price being sought for the security by the seller. Also called the *offer.*

Auction
Public sale of Treasury securities by sealed bids; method of determining the rate or yield.

Basis Point
Smallest unit used in quoting bond yields; equal to 1/100th of a percent (100 basis points equals 1 percent).

Basis Price
The price of a security expressed as a percentage of return on the investment, or yield to maturity.

Bearer Security
A security without the name of the owner on it. The proceeds are payable to the bearer or the person who holds it. Thus, ownership of the securities can be easily transferred. Bearer bonds have been prohibited in the United States since 1982 to help fight money laundering.

Benchmark
A standard used for comparing the performance of bonds of similar maturity. U.S. Treasury securities are considered benchmarks in the global financial market.

Bid
The highest price a buyer is willing to pay. See *ask* price.

Bill
A short-term U.S. Treasury security with a maturity of not more than one year.

Bond
A debt security or IOU with a maturity of more than one year issued for the purpose of raising capital by borrowing. The issuer typically agrees to pay a fixed rate of interest and to repay the principal at maturity.

Bond Equivalent Yield
Converts the simple interest rate on fixed-income securities maturing in less than one year into an annualized yield.

Bond Funds
A mutual fund that concentrates on bonds and that provides investors with a steady income while minimizing the risk to principal.

Bond Insurance
Legal commitment by a third-party insurance company to pay interest and principal installments on a bond issue in the event that the issuer defaults.

Bond Purchase Agreement (BPA)
Contract between an underwriter and an issuer setting out the terms of the sale, including the price of the bonds, the interest rate, and the conditions to closing. Also called the *purchase contract.*

Bond Resolution
Similar to an indenture, a bond resolution provides information about the details of the bond issue, security features, covenants, default events, and other features.

Bond Swap
The sale of one bond and the simultaneous purchase of another, often for the same price.

Bond Year
A way of measuring the average life of an issue, its net interest cost, and its net interest rate. A bond year refers to the number of 12-month intervals there are over a bond's life, measured in $1,000 increments.

Book Entry
Bonds that have no physical certificate. Ownership is maintained in electronic form on a computer. Most U.S. Treasuries use this recordkeeping system.

Broker
A firm or a person who acts as a third party between a buyer and a seller, and offers advice and services to the public. Bond brokers incorporate their fee into the buying and selling price.

Bullet
A noncallable bond that pays a fixed rate of interest and repays the principal upon maturity. Usually pays a lower rate of interest because investors don't have to worry that the bond will be called when interest rates fall.

Call
Actions taken to pay the principal on a bond before the maturity date, in accordance with the issue's call provisions. Also referred to as *redemption provisions.*

Callable
A bond that can be redeemed by the issuer before its maturity date under certain conditions. A premium (a higher price than par value) is normally paid to

the bondholder if this occurs. The main reason for a call is that interest rates have fallen and the issuer wants to refinance its debt at the lower rate.

Call Date
A date prior to maturity at which some bonds may be redeemed by the issuer.

Call Premium
A monetary amount paid by the issuer to exercise a call provision.

Call Price
The price at which a bond can be redeemed or called prior to maturity.

Call Protection
A provision that prevents bonds from being callable for a certain number of years.

Call Risk
The risk that a fall in interest rates will prompt an issuer to redeem callable securities prior to their maturity. As a result, investors may receive a lower rate of interest when they reinvest their principal.

Carry
The interest cost of borrowing funds to finance securities. A positive carry happens when the return from a security is greater than the financing cost. A negative carry is when the financing cost is greater than the return on the securities being financed.

Closed-End Investment Company
An investment company created with a fixed number of shares, which are then traded as listed securities on a stock exchange. After the initial offering, existing shares can only be bought from existing shareholders.

Closing Date
Similar to a *settlement date* but applies to a new issuance of bonds. In the event of a competitively sold issue, the closing may be up to 30 days.

Collateralized Mortgage Obligation (CMO)
A security backed by a pool of mortgage obligations.

Commission
The fee a dealer receives for acting as an agent in a transaction.

Common Stock
A share representing equity ownership in a corporation, which also provides voting rights and entitles the holder to dividends.

Compound Accreted Value
The value of a zero-coupon bond at any given point in time. This includes the principal and accrued compound interest.

Convertible
A type of corporate bond that gives the holder the option to exchange the bond and its remaining coupons for a specified number of common stock shares, usually from the same company.

Convexity
A measure of the rate of change of a debt instrument's sensitivity to interest-rate movements. The term is derived from the convex shape of the graph showing the relationship between a bond's price and its yield. The greater the convexity, the less a bond is affected by interest rates and the higher the price of the bond.

Coupon
The annual amount of interest on a bond that an issuer has promised to pay. If the coupon is blank, it can mean that the instrument is a zero-coupon bond, a new issue, or a variable-rate bond.

Covenant
A part of the bond indenture that offers legal protections to lenders. Covenants can prohibit or require actions by an issuer, such as limiting dividends that are paid or maintaining a certain level of working capital.

Cover Bid
Second-highest bid in an auction sale.

Credit Enhancement
Using the credit of a stronger entity to bolster the credit of a lower-rated entity in bond or note financing. This term is used in the context of bond insurance, bank facilities, and government programs.

Credit Ratings
Rankings issued by ratings agencies that assess an individual or corporation's credit quality.

Credit Spread
A yield difference, typically in relation to a comparable U.S. Treasury security, that reflects the issuer's credit quality. Credit spread also refers to the difference between the value of two securities with similar interest rates and maturities when one is sold at a higher price than the other is purchased.

Current Refunding
A refunding transaction where old bonds are called or mature within 90 days or less of the issuance of the new refunding bonds.

Current Yield
The ratio of interest to the actual market price of the bond, stated as a percentage. For example, a bond with a current market price of $1,000 that pays $60 per year in interest would have a current yield of 6 percent.

Dated (or Issue) Date
The date from which a bond holder is entitled to receive interest, regardless of the date when the bond was actually sold or delivered.

Daycount
The convention used to calculate the number of days in an interest payment period. A 30/360 convention assumes 30 days in a month and 360 days in a year. An actual/360 convention assumes the actual number of days in the given month and 360 days in the year. An actual/actual convention uses the actual number of days in the given interest period and year.

Debenture
Long-term debt instrument that is similar to a bond, except that it is unsecured and backed by the creditworthiness of the borrower and not by collateral.

Debt Limit
Constitutional or statutory limit on the total debt that an issuer may incur.

Debt Service
Principal and interest due on a debt.

Debt-Service Coverage
Indicates a firm's ability to repay a loan. The ratio of net revenues to the debt service requirements.

Debt-Service Requirements
Amount required to service all debts over a specified time period.

Default
Failure to pay principal or interest when due.

Denomination
The face amount of a security or currency.

Derivative
A financial instrument that derives its value from an underlying asset, such as a bond, equity, commodity, or currency. Examples include futures and options.

Discount
The amount (stated in monetary or percentage terms) by which a bond's price trades below its $1,000 par value.

Discount Bond
A bond that sells at below its face value.

Discount Margin
The earned return over a given reference index for a floating rate security.

Discount Note
Short-term promissory notes with a maturity of one year or less issued at a discount over its face value. They have no periodic interest payments.

Discount Rate
The interest rate that the U.S. Federal Reserve charges for short-term loans to its member banks.

Distribution of Principal
Return of principal to unit trust shareholders, usually when a bond reaches maturity, is called, or is sold prior to maturity.

Dollar Bond
A bond quoted in dollar values rather than yield.

Downgrade Risk
Possibility that a bond's rating will be lowered because of deterioration in the issuer's financial condition or the financial condition of a party to the financial transaction.

Duration
Measures the volatility of a bond relative to interest-rate fluctuations. Refers to the percentage change in a bond's price that results from a 1 percent increase or decrease in interest rates. Also known as the *Macaulay Duration*, after economist Frederick Macaulay, who formulated it in 1938.

Embedded Option
Gives the issuer or the bondholder the option to take some action against the other party.

Excess Spread
The net amount of interest payments from underlying assets, less bondholder payments and expenses.

Expected Maturity Date
The date when principal is expected to be paid to investors.

Extension Risk
The risk that rising interest rates will slow anticipated mortgage or loan repayments, tying up investors' money longer than expected and possibly causing them to miss opportunities to earn a higher rate of interest elsewhere.

Face Amount or Value

The par value (i.e., principal) of a bond paid upon redemption. Corporate bonds generally have a par value of US$1,000, municipal bonds US$5,000, and federal bonds US$10,000.

Federal Funds Rate

The interest rate that U.S. banks charge each other for overnight loans to meet their reserve requirements.

Final Maturity Date

The date on which the principal must be paid to investors, which is later than the expected maturity date. Also called *legal maturity date.*

Fixed-Rate Bond

Long-term bond that pays a fixed rate of interest.

Floating-Rate Bond

Bond with an interest rate that fluctuates according to market interest rates or some other index.

Floor

Lower limit for the interest rate on a floating-rate bond.

Flow of Funds

Structure in the bond resolution or trust documents which sets forth the order in which funds generated by an organization will be allocated or channeled.

Forward Cap

An agreement to enter into a cap at some future date.

Forward Floor

An agreement to enter into a floor at some future date.

Forward Swap

An agreement to enter into a swap at some point in the future.

Government-Sponsored Enterprise (GSE)

A group of financing organizations created by the U.S. Congress to enhance the flow of credit to various borrowers, such as homeowners, farmers, and students.

Hedge

Balancing one investment with another to reduce or cancel risk. However, hedging also limits the potential for gain.

High-Yield Bond
Another name for *junk bond*. A high-risk, high-yielding bond with a low credit rating. A speculative bond, as opposed to an investment-grade bond.

I-Bond
An inflation-indexed bond issued by the U.S. Treasury. Series I savings bonds pay a rate of interest that is partly fixed and partly adjusted for inflation.

Indenture
A written agreement between the issuer and its creditors, spelling out the terms of the bond, including interest rate, maturity rate, convertibility, and other details.

Indexed-Rate Bonds
Tax-exempt bonds where the rate is linked to an index, such as the Bond Market Association Swap Index.

Industrial Revenue Bond
A bond issued by a local government agency but backed by the credit of a private enterprise.

Inflation-Adjusted Principal
The principal amount of an inflation-indexed security determined by multiplying the par value by the required index ratio.

Inflation-Indexed Securities
Securities whose principal is adjusted to take into consideration the effects of inflation.

Initial Offering Price
The price at which bonds are first marketed to investors, called the initial offering period.

Insurance
Municipal bond insurance companies insure against default, repaying principal and/or interest, on municipal and certain other types of bonds.

Interest
Payment for the use of money, usually expressed as an annual percentage rate.

Interest-Rate Cap
Also called the *strike rate*, this refers to an agreement where a premium is paid up front or in installments to a counterparty. If the floating interest rate exceeds the stated fixed rate, the counterparty pays the difference. The cap can protect against rising interest rates.

Inverted, or Negative, Yield Curve
An atypical situation where short-term interest rates are higher than long-term interest rates. This usually indicates a business slowdown or a recession on the horizon.

Investment Grade
Safer, high-quality bonds rated BBB or Baa or higher.

IO (Interest-Only) Security
Pays investors only interest and not principal. Such securities are priced at a deep discount to the *notional* principal in calculating the interest due.

Issue
A security that is issued by a government entity or a corporation.

Issue Date
The date when a security is issued or originates.

Issuer
A government, corporation, agency, or supranational organization or other entity that borrows money by issuing a bond.

Junior Security
A junior security ranks below other securities on claims to a corporation's assets and income. For example, common stock is junior to preferred stock.

Junk Bond
A high-risk, high-yielding bond with a low credit rating. A speculative bond as opposed to an investment-grade bond.

Letter of Credit (LOC)
A binding commitment, usually issued by a bank, guaranteeing that the principal and interest will be paid on debt issues if the issuer is unable to do so.

Level Debt Service
A debt-service schedule where annual principal plus interest payments remain approximately the same for the life of the bond. This results in a maturity schedule with increasing principal amounts each year.

Leverage
The use of borrowed money to increase investing power.

LIBOR (London Interbank Offered Rate)
The rate at which banks in the London market charge each other for short-term eurodollar loans.

Line of Credit
A commitment by a bank to provide funds to a borrower, if certain conditions have been met, or if certain conditions do not exist.

Liquidation Value
The amount a securities holder may receive in case of a liquidation of the issuer.

Liquidity
The ability to trade and quickly convert an asset into cash without any price discount.

Lockout
The period of time before the first principal payment is made.

Long-Term Debt
Debt that matures in more than one year.

Manager (or Senior Manager)
The underwriter that serves as the lead underwriter for an account.

Marketability
A measure of a security's ability to be bought or sold on the primary or secondary market.

Market Price or Market Value
For securities traded through an exchange, the last reported price at which a security was sold; for securities traded *over the counter*, the current price of the security in the market.

Maturity Date
The date when the principal, or face amount, is due for payment.

Maturity Schedule
The listing, by dates and amounts, of principal maturities of an issue.

Modified Duration
Macaulay Duration adjusted to price and yield levels to represent the percentage change in the relationship of price and yield.

Monetary Default
Failure to pay principal or interest promptly when due.

Moral Obligation Bond
A type of municipal bond that is backed by a state's *moral* pledge to honor its obligations, rather than a legal one.

Mortgage
A debt instrument in which a loan is used to purchase property and the property, in turn, is the collateral for the loan.

Mortgage-Backed Securities
A security that consists of an interest in a pool of mortgage loans. The principal and interest payments collected from borrowers are passed through to investors.

Mortgage Revenue Bond
A bond issued by a state or local government agency to make or purchase loans for single-family or multifamily residences.

Municipal Bond ("Muni")
Issued by state or local governments for the purpose of financing projects that are in the public interest.

Mutual Fund
Professionally managed pools of money that are set up to meet stated investment goals, which range from growth to income generation to capital preservation.

Negative Convexity
A characteristic of a callable bond in which the principal is returned before maturity when interest rates are declining or after maturity when rates are rising, which may expose investors to the risk of a lower return.

New-Issue Market
Market where companies can raise funds by issuing bonds and notes.

Non-callable Bond
A bond that cannot be called back by the issuer before it matures. Because of the reduced risk, these bonds often offer lower yields.

Non-Investment-Grade
Lower quality bonds rated Baa3 or below by Moody's Investors Service, or BBB− or below by Standard & Poor's. Also called *high-yield bonds.*

Notes
Short-term debt securities, usually with a maturity that is longer than 1 year but less than 10 years.

Notice of Sale
An official document that gives information about an upcoming bond offering and invites bids from underwriters.

Offer
The price at which a seller will sell a security.

Offering Price
The price at which a new issue of securities is offered to investors.

Official Statement (OS)
The prospectus for municipal securities that contains economic, financial, and legal information about the issue.

Option-Adjusted/Effective Duration
Modified duration, which measures the bond's movement for a shift in the yield curve. For noncallable bonds, modified duration and effective duration are the same.

Optional Redemption
A right to retire an issue or a portion of it prior to the stated maturity during a specified number of years.

Order Period
The period during which orders for new issues are placed.

Original Delivery
Also called initial delivery, this refers to the delivery of a new issue to the purchaser, following payment of the purchase price.

Original Face
The face value of a security on its date of issue.

Original-Issue Discount
The difference between a security's price when issued and its face value.

Overcollateralization
Occurs when the amount of collateral used in a given transaction exceeds the principal of the securities issued.

Over-the-counter (OTC) Market
A securities market that is conducted not on a centralized exchange but through dealers who communicate with each other via a network of computers, phones, and faxes.

P&I (Principal and Interest)
Refers to regularly scheduled principal and interest payments or prepayments on mortgage-backed securities.

Par or Par Amount

The face value or principal of a bond or note to be paid at maturity. Also known as *par value.*

Paying Agent

Entity that pays the principal and periodic interest to a bondholder; usually a bank.

Payment Date

The date when principal and interest payments are paid to bond holders.

Performance

The return on an investment.

Perpetual Floating-Rate Note

A floating-rate note with no stated maturity date.

PO (Principal-Only) Security

A security that pays investors principal only and not interest. These are issued at a deep discount from their face value.

Point

One point equals 1 percent of the face value of a bond. For example, 1 point equals $10 on a $1,000 bond.

Pool

A package of mortgage loans or other related financial instruments, which serve as the basis for a security.

Preferred Stock

A class of equity security that is senior to common stock but has no voting rights. Holders of preferred stock have priority over common stockholders in receiving stated dividend amounts and in the liquidation of assets. However, preferred stock is junior to the issuing entity's debt obligations.

Preliminary Official Statement

The initial document of a new municipal securities offering, which does not contain pricing information. Also called a *red herring.*

Premium Bond

Bonds priced greater than par. The opposite of a discounted bond.

Premium or Discount Price

A bond is selling at a premium when its dollar price is greater than its face value. It is selling at a discount when the dollar price is below its face value.

Prepayment
An unscheduled payment made before it is due.

Prepayment Risk
The possibility that a decline in interest rates will cause borrowers to pay off their debts earlier, forcing investors to reinvest at lower prevailing rates.

Price
The cost of a security.

Primary Market (New-Issue Market)
Market where new issues of bonds and notes are first sold to investors by issuers.

Prime Rate
The interest rate that a commercial bank charges its best customers, such as large corporations.

Principal
Amount that a borrower must pay back when the security matures, exclusive of accrued interest. Also called the *par or face value*.

Principal Transaction
A transaction in which the dealer commits its own capital.

Private Label
Term that describes a mortgage security from an issuer that is not a U.S. government agency or U.S. government–sponsored enterprise, such as subsidiaries of investment banks, financial institutions, or homebuilders.

Private Placement
The negotiated sale of new securities to a group of investors, without a public underwriting.

Public Offering Price
The price at which securities are offered for sale to the public.

Put Bond
A bond that allows the investor to sell the bond back to the issuer at a specified price (usually par value) before maturity. An investor might take advantage of this feature if market interest rates were rising.

Rate Reset
The adjustment of the interest rate on a floating-rate security.

Ratings
A grade designating a bond's credit quality. A rating is an evaluation of a bond issuer's financial condition and its ability to make interest payments and to repay the principal as promised. Ratings typically range from AAA (highest quality) to D (default).

Real Interest Rate
An interest rate after deducting the inflation rate so as to reflect the real cost of funds to the borrower and the real yield to the lender.

Real Yield
Inflation-adjusted return on an investment.

Recession
A downturn in economic activity on a large scale. Generally defined as two or more quarters of decline in output, as measured by gross national product (GNP) or gross domestic product (GDP).

Record Date
Date used for determining eligibility in dividend or capital gains distributions or determining the owner who is entitled to the next scheduled payment of principal or interest on a mortgage security.

Redemption
The return of principal to an investor; also, repurchase of investment trust units by the trustee, at the bid price.

Refunding
Using the proceeds from a new bond issue to redeem or retire an outstanding issue.

Registered Bond
A bond whose owner is registered with the issuer or its agent.

Registered Owner
Name of the holder of a security who receives principal and interest payments on the record date.

Reinvestment Risk
Possibility that interest income or principal repayments will have to be reinvested at lower rates as a result of declining interest rates.

Revenue Bond
A bond on which the debt service is payable solely from the revenue generated from the public-works projects (highways, bridges, stadiums, and so on) being financed.

Risk
A measure of the degree of uncertainty and/or of financial loss inherent in an investment or decision.

Round Lot
The normal trading unit of a security. Block of bonds of US$100,000 or higher.

Scale
Listing by maturity of the price or yields at which a new issue will be offered.

Secondary Market
The market where investors can buy and sell securities after they have been underwritten by an investment bank and issued on the primary market.

Secured Debt
A debt guaranteed by specific assets or a lien. If the borrower defaults, lenders have the right to sell the assets to meet their claims.

Security
Revenue sources or collateral pledged to repay a bond.

Selling Group
A selling group consists of dealers or brokers who have been invited to participate in the offer of a new issue of securities, but neither share in the profits of the syndicate nor are responsible for any unsold amounts.

Senior Securities
Any security that has priority over other securities in terms of claims or liquidation. For example, bonds are considered senior to common stock.

Serial Bonds
An issue of bonds that matures gradually in consecutive years.

Servicing
Collecting payments and interest from borrowers, maintaining payment records and tax records, and delinquency loan follow-up, among other functions.

Settlement Date
The date for the delivery of securities and payment of funds.

Short
Borrowing and then selling securities that one does not own, in anticipation of a price decline. When prices fall, the short is *covered* by buying the securities back and returning them to the lender.

Short-Term Debt
Generally, a bond with a maturity of one year or less. Maturities of up to three years may still be considered short-term debt.

Sinker
A bond with a sinking fund.

Sinking Fund
A fund in which money is set aside in order to retire various kinds of debt.

Sponsor
An investment firm that organizes a unit investment trust and offers the units for sale.

Spread
(1) The difference between the price at which an issue is purchased from an issuer and the price at which it is reoffered by the underwriters to the first holders. (2) The difference in price or yield between two securities.

Stated Maturity
The last possible date on which the last payment of the longest loan may be paid.

STRIPS
Acronym for Separate Trading of Registered Interest and Principal of Securities. A U.S. Treasury security whose coupons are separated from the principal and which are sold as zero-coupon bonds. They are issued at a deep discount from par and mature at par. STRIPS pay no interest.

Subordinated Debt
A debt of lower priority that pays interest and principal but only after interest has been paid on senior debt.

Surety Bond
A contract in which one party guarantees that a second party will fulfill an obligation or contractual promises to a third party. If the second party fails to meet the obligation, the third party is entitled to recover its losses via the surety bond.

Swap
The sale of one security and the simultaneous purchase of another with the proceeds, usually for the same price and often done for tax purposes.

Syndicate
A group of investment firms, banks, insurers, and others who work together to sell a new investment to the public.

Take-Down
The discounted price at which members of an underwriting account are allowed to buy bonds from the account.

Taxable Municipal Bond
A municipal bond whose interest is not eligible for tax-exempt status on federal income taxes. This is because it is issued for purposes that are deemed not to offer a significant benefit to the public.

Tax Base
The total property and resources subject to taxation. (Also known as *assessed valuation*.)

Tax-Exempt Bond
Generally, a municipal bond whose interest payments are excluded from the gross income of holders for federal income tax purposes, and sometimes state and local taxes.

Tax-Exempt Commercial Paper
A short-term loan issued for periods up to 270 days that offers some tax-exempt provisions.

Tax-Exempt/Taxable Yield Equivalent Formula
A formula that converts the yield on a tax-exempt bond into the yield on a taxable bond to see whether it's more profitable on an after-tax basis to invest in the tax-exempt debt obligation.

T-Bill Rate
The weekly average auction rate of the three-month Treasury bill stated as the bond-equivalent yield.

Technical Default
A violation of the bond indenture terms, other than failure to pay interest or principal, such as not maintaining the required reserves.

Term Bond
Debt security that has a single maturity date.

Term Funding
Financing undertaken to meet specific cash needs over a specific period of time.

Total Return
A figure showing how well an investment has performed, usually over a one-year period. It takes into consideration any increase or decrease in the price of the security as well as income from dividends and interest.

Trade Date
The date on which a trade, sale, or purchase occurs, with settlement to be made later.

Tranche
A French word meaning "slice." With bonds, it refers to an offering of a specific class of bonds, such as mortgages, which have varying degrees of risk within that class.

Transfer Agent
An agent employed to maintain shareholder records; to cancel and issue certificates; and to handle issues relating to lost, destroyed, or stolen certificates.

Transparency
The concept of disseminating price, volume, and other information to the public.

Treasury Inflation-Protected Securities (TIPS)
Treasury Inflation Protected Securities are issued by the U.S. Treasury and are identical to other U.S. government bonds except that the coupon payments and principal are automatically adjusted to keep pace with inflation. In exchange for that protection, the bond offers a lower interest rate.

True Interest Cost
A method of calculating bids on new issues of municipal securities that takes the time value of money into consideration.

True Yield
The rate of return to the investor taking into account the payment of capital gains at maturity on a bond bought at a discount.

Trustee
An individual or organization appointed by a bond issuer who represents the bondholders and ensures that the bond issuer complies with the terms of the indenture.

Undated Issue
A floating-rate note with no stated maturity date.

Underwriter
A securities dealer (usually an investment bank) that acts as an intermediary between a corporation or municipality that is issuing a bond and the investors to whom it is sold.

Unit
A fractional, undivided interest in a unit investment trust.

Unit Investment Trust
Passively managed fund that invests in a fixed parcel of bonds, which are held in trust until maturity.

Volatility
A statistical measure of the variance of price or yield over time.

Yield
The annual rate of return, or income, received from an investment, usually expressed as a percentage. The yield refers to the dividends or interest received.

Yield Curve
The graphical representation of the relationship between yield and maturity among bonds of different maturities and the same credit quality. This line shows the term structure of interest rates.

Yield Spread
Differences in yields between various debt securities. The spread offers a means of comparing financial products.

Yield-to-Call
Yield that an investor would receive on a bond that is called before maturity.

Yield to Maturity (YTM)
The average annual return that an investor would receive if the security is held until the maturity date. The calculation includes total coupon payments, reinvestment of interest, current market price, and time to maturity.

Yield-to-Worst
The lowest yield on a callable bond redeemed before maturity or the lowest yield to maturity.

Zero-Coupon Bond
A bond for which no periodic interest payments are made and on which the full face value is paid on maturity.

INDEX

A

B

C

D

E

F

G

H

I

J

K

L

M

N

O

P

R

S

T

U

V

W

Y

Z